Manifest West

Different Roads

Traversing the Diverse Roads of the West

Manifest West

Different Roads

Traversing the Diverse Roads of the West

Western
Press Books

WESTERN PRESS BOOKS
GUNNISON, COLORADO

ISBN: 978-1-60732-364-8

Library of Congress Control Number: 2014943430
Published in the United States of America

Western Press Books
Gunnison, Colorado

"Prayer For Rain" by Harrison Candelaria Fletcher was originally published in *Broad Street: A Magazine Of True Stories*, Issue 2.1 Spring/Summer 2014.

"The Passage of Wild Horses" by John Haggerty previously appeared in Issue 11 of *High Desert Journal* in the spring of 2010.

"Bison I" by Chad Hanson also appears in *Patches of Light: Prose Poems* (Chad Hanson, Red Dragonfly Press, 2014, p. 41).

"Resistance" by Ellaraine Lockie first appeared in *Plainsongs* in 2007.

"The Bones That Were Our People" by C. L. Prater was previously published in *The Wayfarer: A Journal of Contemplative Literature*, Vol. 1 Issue. 1, September, 2012.

"Wherever the Road Goes" by Mark Rozema was originally published in the Fall 2013 issue of *Superstition Review*, an online journal from Arizona State University.

"Chinese Dream on the Canadian Border" by Scott Starbuck first appeared in the FutureCycle Press Anthology: *American Society: What Poets See* in 2012.

"Grandpa Lupe" by Alex L. Swartzentruber was first published in *Canvas Magazine* in the spring of 2010.

"Six Feet Under the Prairie" by Tim Weed originally appeared in *Colorado Review*, Summer 2004.

"John True Arrow" by Sarah Brown Weitzman was previously published in *Riversedge*, Vol. XVI, #1, 2002.

EDITOR

LARRY K. MEREDITH

ASSOCIATE EDITORS

LAURA ANDERSON

JENNIFER GAUTHIER

A.J. STERKEL

ASSISTANT EDITORS

CRAIG ALLEN

MELANIE BECIC

LINDSIE CONKLIN

A. J. HANCE

SAM HIRT

MADISON HOWARD

ALEX JENSEN

M. K. KASUNIC

MONICA LEWIS

BECCA LUBANG

ALLEN TRAN

BECKY YOUNG

CONSULTING EDITORS

RUSSELL DAVIS

DAVID ROTHMAN

MARK TODD

COVER AND INTERIOR DESIGN

SONYA UNREIN

COVER PHOTOGRAPH

JACK MEREDITH

CONTENTS

FICTION

NON-FICTION

CONTRIBUTORS

Manifest West

Different Roads

Traversing the Diverse Roads of the West

Larry K. Meredith

Foreword

"Different roads sometimes lead to the same castle."
—George R.R Martin

When the editors of this anthology began contemplating a 2014 theme, our deliberations uncovered a wide diversity of ideas. So there it was, right in front of us, perfectly exposed and absolutely dead-on. "Diversity" it was. Western Diversity. Our anthology would lay bare the variety of people, geography, ideologies, wildlife, weather, histories, and maybe even attitudes toward tourists along with much more of what makes up this part of the United States. The possibilities were endless, as we discovered when we received nearly four hundred submissions from authors across the country.

The editors were impressed with, not only the variety of topics covered in the submissions of poetry, short fiction and creative non-fiction, but also with the skill the authors demonstrated as they tackled the theme with enthusiasm, humor, wistfulness, and wonderful creativity.

Descriptions of the diverse nature of the West are endless and . . . yes, diverse. Here's an example.

Not long ago a western Colorado newspaper published a letter from a woman who complained about encountering a herd of cattle being driven to or from the high country on a well-used highway. The woman was concerned about the smell and the resulting mess on her car. This is a common occurrence in rural areas of the state. Traffic jams near small towns are often the result of those herds of cattle being patiently prodded by cowboys and cowgirls from summer range to winter feeding, and back again in the spring.

I wrote about this incident in a column for the *Denver Post*. I had been named a "Colorado Voice" and invited to submit several columns over the course of a year. I gave this column the title "Defined by Cow Poop on the Road." When it appeared in a Sunday edition, however, the title had been changed to "Defined by Road Apples."

Well, shucks, every self-respecting Westerner knows that "road apples" are left by horses and not by cattle. I received a couple of letters telling me I was in error and had to reply that some big-city editor representing a class of immigrants from obviously "non-Western" states had made the change and that it wasn't my fault.

Both incidents—the complaint of the letter-writer and the editor's unwitting error—are illustrative of the kind of "diversity" found throughout the part of the United States we call the "West."

The letter-writer (from Aspen or its environs) was evidently not familiar with Western ways, including our ranchers' need to move cattle the shortest distance from point A to point B. She may well have been a part-time resident more attuned to city driving on four-lane roads without potholes and certainly without the residue of passing herds of animals.

The *Denver Post* editor can be forgiven for his or her use of the term "road apples." Perhaps the paper's policies prohibited the use of the word "poop" or maybe it was a space issue. Or maybe a deadline loomed. Nevertheless he or she should have known better.

Reacting to the woman's letter, I wrote that the cowboys and cowgirls she saw herding the cattle "are who we used to be." I also said that the woman and other drivers who disliked meeting cattle on the roads "represent who we've become."

This story illustrates, in a small way, the changes the West has undergone in the past several decades and the area's increasingly diverse population, attitudes, races, businesses, lifestyles, cultures and aspirations.

This issue of *Manifest West* includes outstanding writing from 27 authors representing the whole of America (and even one from Canada). Their locales are as diverse as their subjects. From Vermont to California, they write about wildfire and drought, deserts and mountains, history and current events. From Arizona to Canada, they consider the assimilation of Chinese and Mexican immigrants, life in cities and small towns, changes that affect ways of life and the eternal changelessness of some aspects of the American West.

The works in this anthology reflect both the myth and the truth about the part of the United State we call the "West." Is there one "true" West? Or have the changes that are overwhelming most of the rest of the country so modified the West that there is little commonality?

The editors of *Manifest West* believe, with Stephen R. Covey, that our "strength lies in differences, not in similarities," and we are constantly amazed by what Stanley Baldwin calls "the many-sidedness of truth."

Many sides of the truth of the West are represented herein. Is everything here absolutely the truth? You decide.

POETRY

Nina Bennett

Register Cliff, Wyoming

Names incised in the rock face
like signatures in a museum guest book.
Dirt swirls, sticks to my legs,
coats my sneakers as I circle the landmark,
search for indentations left in the limestone
over a hundred years ago
by people in pursuit of a dream
or trying to outrun a demon.
I kneel, press my palm over the wagon
wheel rut carved into the earth.
Buffalo bellow and snort;
the ground quivers beneath my hand
as the herd moves in unison.
Muffled moans of a woman in labor,
breathing measured as she attempts to delay
the birth until the protection of that night's camp
is reached. Praying for the safe arrival of her first child,
she wants only to feel the weight in her arms
as her baby seeks the comfort of her breast.
She will wrap her son in a quilt
stitched during months of travel.

I crouch by the eroded ruts.
My fingers palpate the earth, take the pulse
of those who passed here long before.
The burden of unfulfilled promises,
endings and beginnings.
Prairie grass sways as the Oregon Trail
merges into the horizon, a discernible
break where the weight of wagons

left its mark, a permanent gouge
in the soul of the plains.
Blood courses through my fingertips
as I release the dirt back to the ground,
unable to distinguish my heartbeat
from that of the past.

Peter Bridges

Rancher

Lean man on strong brown mare dislikes the towns,
Fears cities whence crass millions may come camp
On his high fragile pastures. He rides rock crowns
Of mountains, turns home tired by moon's mild lamp.
The rancher tells the moon that he is tired
Of snows, and taxes, worries over prices,
And fending off developers. He's fired
Two hands for drugs; no place seems safe from vices.
The rancher's son is bored and surfs the Web,
The rancher's wife dreams winter on a beach,
The rancher's love of country is at ebb
But he thinks of how his father used to teach
That we can create paradise again
Below these peaks, on this high flowering plain.

Joe Carvalko

County Road 80

Between Cordova and Truchas,
el hombre
looks skyward, wizened,
blinded by the sun's flux,
in honor of that birth-marked
wiry muscled
clan clawing desiccated soil
from an Iberian enclave,
where Aramaic
voices echoed in ancient temples,
Sephardic fathers' fathers
escaped
clinging
to moth-eaten lanyards
put out to sea, westerly,
to navigate the flotsam
of leftover queens, conquistadors,
of fame, gold, salvation,
that collapsed
una civilización,
a demise not dignified by glorious battle
or solemn mass, but wasted,
waiting to dispose those in monk's clothes,
those who plundered and stole, tomes, trinkets,
el número cero,
never to gain the language.
El hombre lives,
crypt-like,
Shabbat candle-waiting stars, salted meat,
middle-rooms swept, linen cloth and spices

winding the dead,
their names buried in graves across
l'arroyo,
on County Road 80
between
Cordova and Truchas
invincible, he remains—
mi abuelo.

William Cordeiro

Land of Enchantment

Past a busted ghost-
town's cobbled ribs,
a river's disappeared
down arroyos, sinks,

pink oxidized slopes
flashing by. Far dust-
devils blackout noon.
Strata burnt to crust;

rock rut straddles sand;
wells with water-tables
leveled & dry. Rubbled
fence posts & a token

outhouse, hogans, geo-
desic domes & junked
tin shacks shucked &
truckled under jinxed

flat lines: Sun mars
a far, charred hard-
scrabble that gravels
over miles sparse

with sage. The coyotes
lope across more veins
of ravaged strip-mines;
& one pure white horse

has escaped its fence
to nibble on parched
roadside grass, a last
survivor of the hills,

which in the sunset
over mountains lets
all the sky catch fire
in its flouncing mane.

David Lavar Coy

Cowboys Explore

When we thought ourselves first
to traverse the draw,
one of a hundred
that sprawls down the valley,
we stumbled amazed
onto an ancient grave,

and when we figured
we alone had climbed
to the top of the peak,
we found a tin heart
on a leather string,
the kind lovers keep,

and when exploring
a cave, we crawled on our knees
down a crack to an open cavern.
Hard to believe
a crowd of Chinese tourists
watched with flashlights

what must have seemed our births.

Chad Hanson

Bison I

The state of Montana hosts a bison hunt. Shooters apply, and then they hold a lottery. A family from Indiana wins. They drive their truck toward a herd. Today, the honor goes to the first son. He targets a bull that's walking point to protect women and yearlings. The bison trembles. Then he falls. The father pumps an elbow. Siblings jump. The mother hides a tear of pride. They walk up to the bull and find his chest heaving. This time, the father shoots a handgun from a holster tucked under his nylon coat. The herd watches at a distance. They can feel the weight of the scenario. The spirit of North America, dead at the feet of seven consumers from Bloomington.

Duane L. Herrmann

Next Five Exits

On the small state Highway,
 one-seventy-seven
to be exact,
 and rural all the way,
the sign says,
 when entering town:
"Mattfield Green –
 Next Five Exits."

The town has five streets
 that cross the highway
so all are "exits"
 into the town,
just like any respectable
 metro region!

Who says country
 has no sense of humor?
Big City: stick it
 to your self-importance!

M.E. Hope

Conceptual Models of Geomorphology for
Cutoffs on the Sprague River

The water doesn't know the science,
the channel doesn't care, only the hydrologist
ponders the formula and graphs.

We believe we own the sky,
believe that land and its names
were waiting for the right shade of eyes
to view its potential. It is holy in ways
we need, and we find ourselves absorbed
by the sanctity that comes from discovery
naming mountains, telling rivers
their roil and course.

We decide which animal should exist
tossing aside species like rice.
And in the long history of want,
we people and un-people,
men and women. We move,
annihilate, diminish to the extent they
become a percentage of human.
And then in the history books,
in the lengthy list of accomplishments
we ignore those footnotes.

Tell the river where it should go
and you can almost hear laughter.
In the land's long memory
we are a flicker of shadow
at the edge of a dream
that is forgotten upon waking.

William Hudson

Assimilation

And old Hildo told me
As we stood three-deep
At the Pan Cigar Store,
Waiting our turn at the bar

For a cheap wine wake-me-up,
Six in the morning,
On the way to the orchards—

And he told me in his shy way
How, after Pearl Harbor,
He and another Filipino
Ran up to an Asian man

They thought Japanese,
Right there on Wapato's
Main Street, and hit him,

Yelling, "What have you done?"

And the Japanese man
Turned out to be Korean.

Marc Janssen

Fixed Points in California

Canyon Country
>
> The pink tiled roofs
> Washed away from us
> And down the hill to
> Break on the shore of
> The Antelope Valley Highway.
>
> There was piano music
> In the backyard
> As the professor and his
> Wife shared a cool beer.

We like to think of homes as fixed points
Secure compass readings

Oxnard
>
> In the fifties
> The stucco ranch houses
> Must have been something . . .
> Not now, with ten people
> Living in each.
>
> Anonymous pulsing bass
> Pulls up to the corner
> Someone without a face
> Walks to the car window
> Then steps away.

But are actually transient, moving
Recklessly changing direction

Oakland
>> From BART's flickering window
>> Away from the rubble of the Nimitz freeway
>> The lightless remains of stately homes
>> Gutted, and carved up.

>> It is quiet here
>> A far away siren serenade;
>> A van from the electric company
>> Steals down the street toward Berkley.

Homes are a neighborhood's complexion
As constant as eyeliner

Don Kunz

Big Hat Country

Rapid City, Ruidoso, Bozeman,
Eagle Pass, Marfa, Yuma, Odessa,
Cortez, Tombstone, Wichita,
Deadwood, Durango, Dodge.

Sloped, vented, antiqued,
Shapeable, crushable, packable.
Sun shade, rain cover, fly swatter,
Water bucket, feed trough.

Stetson, Justin, Tony Lama, Bailey's,
Beaver Brand, Monte Carlo, Double S,
Larry Mahan, Dorfman Pacific, Minnetonka,
Resistol, Rodeo King, Charlie 1 Horse.

Felt, fur, nubuck,
Bullhide, cowhide, canvas,
Straw, palm leaf, seagrass,
Shantung, 6 X wool.

Mustang, Cheyenne, Rancher,
Pinchfront, Silverbelly, Outback,
Quarter Horse, Brush Hog, Gus,
Pistol Pete, Batwing, Hondo.

Hill country cowboys, rodeo bunnies,
Wagon masters, drifters, desperadoes,
Night riders, card sharps, Texas Rangers,
Rebel souls, high steppers, electric Navahos.

Ellaraine Lockie

Resistance

The Native American saloon
on the one-block Montana Main Street
was the only authorized place for them
Outside of Rocky Boy Indian Reservation

My visiting adolescent daughters
Ever-vigilant defenders of diversity
crossed the race barrier

Laid their benevolence on the bar
along with money for beer
on a busy Saturday night

Dead silence ensued
in a bar room pre-brawl-like scene
Resurrected from a John Wayne flick
and played on a present day reel

Casting the daughters' bewilderment
at the reverse discrimination
And the community's discomfort with
the arriving flight of left wingers

Rebecca Pelky

California Zephyr, Westbound

What I see through the glass are vistas; how at sunrise
the mist glows like wildfire, lighting the cut stone in orange,
and the pines. How the scattered herds of reddish cows
amble in lines across high pastures. The train tears me away
before I can even say I was there, pressed against the glare
like a sideshow, each view a flashbulb echo on my inner eye,

the way, if you stare at the sun, then close your eyes,
you'll see them repeated in red, then blue.
Or, open your eyes wide as you're pulled through
a tunnel under tons of rock, and you'll still see
the skyline of sunrise and red pines as you catch your breath
and wait in the dark to come out the other side. Somewhere,
Muir is climbing a tree in a windstorm, or scalding in sulfur
at 30 below, because he heard empty, but found infinite.

Scot Siegel

Epistles to the Imnaha Pack:
Dispatches from Journey

*In December 2011 'Journey' (aka 'OR-07'), an alpha male, was the
first wild gray wolf to enter California in eighty-seven years.*

1.
Comrades. I've traversed
Century. Beetle-kill. Dammed
Tributary. Paved marsh. Old
Hunting grounds. I've slept
In culvert back of ranch feedlot,
Where county agent smoke
In white truck, and clutch old
Nemesis (gun). But look away.

Last night I lift leg over chain
At rest stop pop machine.
Caretaker slept in bullet-shaped
Den on wheels. Strange,
This world's never felt so real;
Our kind's never been so alive!

2.
I remember ringnecks
Easy chukars we'd poach.
Non-natives. But sweet!
I remember fields of thistle
And wheat, where we took
A fawn in full stride, just for
Sport. Then dipped our muzzles
Into the cool riffles of Umatilla . . .

I've trekked so far—Wallowas
Blues. Siskiyous. Shasta—
Just to mark a few old friends:
Live Oak with gnarled waist;
Ruddy face of Bull Pine; and Redwoods,
whose fine pubis I find so arousing.

3.
Now I hunker in gravel of interstate
Shoulder. Let gloom sickle moon
Slide over my neck, and listen:
Mangy cousin, Coyote croons.
Black bear rummages dumpster
At state park. I take no part,
Comrades—I have no patience
For their ways: A sacrilege!—

I am not content to gorge on
The still-warm hare, sleek hawk hoists,
Then drops, mid-flight, like charity . . .
I am more focused now: I track a new
Scent: Plot each step like
A sacrament.

4.
Comrades. It is late. Solstice
Chills me. I'm lonely, yes. I long
For licks on my slate coat—
Tonight, I'll summon what's left
Of our pack of ghosts. Huddle below
Bridge abutment. Sing to the long-
Extinct stars: The night is so bleak,
Yet beautiful!—

We have come so far—
Someday, this country will be ours again
I thought I heard Ishi
Whisper to me in a dream.
Comrades, the world is not what it seems.
I know she is out there somewhere . . .

Jared Smith

Front Range on Fire

The mountains are coming on us
are filling the lungs   or
they are retreating from stone
heavy as ghost flesh,   wispy
lives choking out life everywhere.

A woman sitting beneath a piñon tree
feels wind separate strands of her hair
until her scalp itches, moves her
gray skirt over snow-white thigh, passing
over her nipples in their cashmere nest,
warm globes and without words reaches
into her purse, her long delicate boned fingers
feeling for anything lost in the smoke within.

How many fires light the Front Range states?
I am talking of the fire within you
that fills books and musical interludes
swirling upward and outward forever,
and I am talking of the fire outside you
that rages in the empty beds of your house
and all the houses along your ridge,
and I am speaking of the fire outside
that is breathed into your lungs from pine
and exploded homes of cedar whose walls
now contain the immensity of what is beyond,
how many fires that the media reports
and how many others they fear to dream of?
How many keys empty of their locks?

Scott T. Starbuck

Chinese Dream on the Canadian Border

I have two books: the Bible
and Kesey's *Sometimes a Great Notion*,
and the guard says
"只有一本书"
translation: "Only one book!"

The language of the Bible
is trees, mountains, rivers,
and can never be destroyed
so, Lord forgive me,
I choose Kesey's book.

Its torso river cover
looks like the Siletz in Oregon
where I trolled for sea-run cutthroats
between the Movie House
below Coyote Rock
and my deckhand Tristan's house
on Siletz Bay.

Maybe I choose the book because
Merry Prankster Kesey
was a Coyote too, of sorts,
symbolic, trickster, appearing
as an omen, vanishing in thickets
like his character Hank Stamper who said
"And if Oregon was to get into it
with California I'd fight for Oregon."

Now California, Oregon, and
Washington all speak Chinese,
and I wonder aloud
"How long before Mt. Rushmore
has the face of '黄帝?"
translation: "Yellow Emperor?"
"Already does," says the guard in English.

In Kesey's book there is a disoriented deer
swimming out to sea
like throngs of migrants to Canada,
two languages of man,
visceral and wise,
Heart of the Pacific Northwest
that changes all invaders,
gift and sacrifice and renewal beyond
anyone's wildest dreams.

Alex L. Swartzentruber

Grandpa Lupe

On my 15th birthday
Grandpa Lupe sang
from a silver harmonica.
The metal in his palm
became a mariachi band
when he brought it to his lips.
That's when I really began
to curse my mother
for never learning Spanish,
never passing it on to me,
never taking us to Mexico
to see the family.

I wonder if Grandpa ever felt the same
about never learning Chinese.
His father was a quiet man
from across the choppy Pacific.
Yellow plus brown makes more brown.
Or that's how assimilation goes in Tampico,

but when Grandpa and I go out to eat,
we don't go to the Mexican joint.
We eat egg rolls,
lo mein,
and rice without beans.

Pepper Trail

Hydrology, Northern Great Basin

Breathe
Breathe in
The waters recede
Shorelines rise and stand
Terraces, shelves and sills
Mark their centuries of shore
In these mudstones are footprints
Asterisks of bird, paws of cougar and wolf
Then, heavy heels and broad toes, strange marks of men

But the breath cannot be held forever, and so breathe out
The slow moist exhalation of ice in its melting
Big-bellied clouds rising over mountains
Epoch of returning rain, pluvial
Refilling the ancient lakes
Lahontan, Bonneville
Water mirrors sky
Breathe out
Breathe

Miles Waggener

Phoenix Eclogue

I asked the man at the counter if Corona Light
came in packs bigger than twelve in the walk-in cooler.
You mean the beer cave? I doubt it. But you could look.
Need to help the people behind you. I'll meet you in there.
I pushed through the door of the walk-in
and heard a rustling like mice in grain.
And towering inside the beer cave
stood the equestrian statue of King Philip III of Spain.
It was in my way. But something tired and nimble thrashed
and stirred inside the bronze steed and monarch.
It was hard to squeeze around its forelegs
to look for Corona cases (which are a much better deal
than the twelvers). But I had to stop and admire the horse
and rider, which should be at the center
of the Plaza Mayor in Madrid, but
was now in the walk-in cooler of the Circle K
on Cave Creek and Peoria Road in Phoenix.
But what was that sound? The twitches of an insect
trapped in the inner ear? Once, my friend John
was waiting for his table at the Red Lobster
when something flew in his ear and we
had to go to the emergency room, where they
pulled out a cricket. A cricket inside a grown man's ear.
Crickets don't fly said the ER doctor. It must have been in his hair.
A little passenger, said the nurse.
I plugged and unplugged my ears. Then I
figured it out. When Giovanni de Bologna
and Pietro Tacca crafted their statue in 1616,
the horse's teeth were parted around
the monarch's bit, for the sculpted horse loved

its master's bridle. And so it was de Bologna and Tacca,
by employing the lost wax method, opened
the teeth of the metal horse in mid-Piaffe,
bringing the muzzle toward its chest,
creating a lifelike aperture in the statue.
But swifts, exhausted from their trans-hemispheric
migration, took it for a nesting nook, as they do
gutters or roof tiles. Once past the teeth, the birds
lost their way and tumbled into its hollow belly.
How generations of trapped birds
had heard the flute and ankle bells of buskers and fire eaters,
or the inquisition's spectacle in the plaza. These last
remaining birds would now hear people
buying boxes of Michelob Ultra. Consider
the horse frozen in place, perennially unoccupied
for the starvation of swifts until now. Think of the voyage
from the tip of Africa to Plaza Mayor, how swifts sleep
in midflight, change their body temperature during storms
crossing the Mediterranean. I was thinking about this
when the clerk finally joined me. Any luck?
No, but nice statue. Pretty cool, eh?
We just put that in here for the Super Bowl.
It's from Spain. I know. Are those birds?
Yeah. They said they'd quiet down. I bet
you didn't expect to see this in here. No, I really didn't.
It's okay. No one does.

Sarah Brown Weitzman

John True Arrow

They who once rivaled the clouds in meanings
of many smokes and brought down buffalo

are now reserved on a granted ground
where in the town his wife, Laughing Eyes,

is called Maria and he is just a Johnny.
Here they drag themselves like broken ponies

to force a poor soil that sucks the color
from their lives and yields finally this pale stuff.

Here they've become old but not elders.
Here their sons drink in new tradition.

Here their daughters lie with pay-day men
from the factories where the mocking smoke

of the white man's waste rises up and roams free
mindless and mute to massacre the earth.

FICTION

John Haggerty

The Passage of Wild Horses

He found the horse about three-quarters up one of those canyons that cut the desert mountain ranges like ragged wounds. It was a brown-and-white mare from one of the wild herds that roam around like moving fossils, artifacts of the mean, drunken miners, the benighted settlers, the outright lunatics who brought their animals to this angry land.

The men and women were mostly gone. They left behind not just the old, abandoned, and rotting shacks, dead and wind-scoured orchards, collapsing tunnels, and other mummified human dreams, but their animals as well. And it seemed they had formed their horses and donkeys in their own image because they possessed the same iron-headed obstinacy that made them all, humans and animals, unsuitable for life back East, for the softness that comes in places where regular rain gives life an illusion of predictability. Their animals were somehow more than them, because they stayed in the desert long after the last of the hard-rock derelicts shuffled off to slow, drunken deaths in the cities on the coasts.

He hadn't seen the animals much, just traces: hoofprints, dried dung. But every once in a while he would get a glimpse of the real thing, a herd of wild horses, a dozen at the most, kicking up dust, a cyclone of vitality in the bare, brown land. He would always stop, sit in his battered old Jeep to watch them move across the hot, empty land, and it felt like looking into a mirror. The last of the wild horses and the last of the prospectors, both of them looking for things increasingly rare—a long, silent day, an unfettered breath, the mirage of an easy life.

Something in that side canyon had caught his eye, drawn him up there for the very first time. The sedimentation suggested a vague hint of mineral wealth. It wasn't much, probably another false lead like most things in his life, but worth a try anyway. As he walked he found his mind moving repeatedly to the letter in his shirt pocket. His sister in Oregon, her children moved out.

She asked him to come live with her, to give up his baking trailer, the dying Jeep, the pointless deprivation and empty isolation of desert life.

Preoccupied as he was, he had missed the signs of animal activity: the disturbed brush, the piles of manure that announced that a herd was nearby. But then a mile up inside those gritty limestone and mud walls, there the horse was.

He stopped still when he saw it, not wanting to spook it, surprised and enchanted at such an unusual sight. But soon he realized there was something wrong. For one thing, it appeared to be alone. The wild horses were herd animals, always traveling in groups. And the horse barely moved at the sound of his footsteps. It leaned up against the rough canyon wall, head hung low. He saw that it was not weighting its left foreleg. It was hard to tell from where he was, but he guessed that it had broken a bone. A veterinarian had once told him that horses were perfect animals except for their legs and digestive systems, the joke being that there wasn't much to a horse besides that. He figured that this must be the way many of them die—a misstep in a rocky canyon and then abandonment by the herd to a painful and lonely end.

It wasn't the first time he had seen imminent death. Death, he figured, was what the world was about, and the desert had no problem rubbing your face in it. The desert is a kind of museum of death, preserving its traces in the sand as in glass cases. But something in him rebelled against this one. Maybe it was the rarity of the wild horse or its beauty or its ties to the past. Or just the deep sadness of death coming to it in this way, left alone for perhaps the first time in its life.

He could see now that the horse was a female, probably not too old, maybe a couple of years. He quietly sat down in the wash about 30 feet away. It nervously twitched its head and moved restively on its three good legs, tentatively setting down the injured leg as if to run but immediately taking the weight back off.

He unscrewed the lid of his canteen to take a drink, pondering what to do. Smelling the water, the horse's head came up, its nostrils expanding to take more air in. He watched the animal, thinking, and then moved toward it slowly, his canteen held before him. The horse snorted and tossed its head but remained staring at the canteen, even as he got close enough to pour the contents onto a dished rock beneath the horse's nose. He backed away and the horse buried its nose in the water, snuffling it greedily.

He ran back down the canyon. It was a couple of miles to his Jeep, and the day was hot. He was sweating and tired when he got back to the horse, carrying a gallon can of water and a plastic garbage bag. Once again he opened the water container so the horse could smell it, keeping its attention while he arranged the garbage bag over some rocks, making a crude tub. Moving carefully, he poured the water out for the horse. It almost pushed him aside with its head as it reached for the water. He backed away and watched it drink desperately from the makeshift trough.

The next day he came back with more water and a bale of hay. It was a little hotter that day, even in the relative cool of the canyon, and the horse again drank greedily. He spread the hay out next to it and it ate quickly. He sat down a ways off and watched it with a mixture of pleasure and concern. There was really no way for him to help this animal, he knew. He wasn't a vet, but he was pretty sure that it had broken a fetlock, a death sentence for any horse, domestic or wild. He couldn't get it down the canyon, and even if he could, there would be no way to repair the damage. But he loved its still-smooth coat, its deep, brown eyes, its untameability.

After the horse ate it hobbled around a bit, eying him warily. He sat still, trying to silently communicate his good intentions to an animal that had never felt such things as human generosity or openness in a harsh life full of fear and want.

He never tried to touch it in the days that followed. That felt too presumptuous or unclean—that he would exact such a price for water and food, things that were easy for him. He would just look at it, letting its wildness soak into him, take him away from the dreary lives of men.

After a week it stopped eating hay, so he brought oats. It only ate the oats for a day before it stopped eating completely. Two days later it stopped drinking water. He sat as before, silently watching, and saw for the first time its dull coat, the growing lifelessness in its eyes, the resigned sag in its neck. The next day he returned with a .45.

The horse didn't even move now as he walked toward it. It leaned against the canyon wall, its head drooping. He moved as close to it as he ever had, close enough for a single, sure shot. He raised the revolver, almost touching its barrel to the horse's forehead. The animal stirred, lifting its head as if to look at him one last time. Later he would tell himself it was just foolish sentimentality, but he thought, in that instant, that he saw a sadness and an acceptance in its eyes, a weariness of suffering, a profound exhaustion. He stood there holding the gun for a long time until the weight caused his shoulder to burn and his hand to shake. The horse stayed unmoving and impassive, even as he lowered the gun and turned away. He saw his mistake then, interfering as men always do, with the best intentions, claiming ownership where there was none, applying rules to lawlessness, trying to make everything up in his own image, making rights and wrongs out of events far beyond such feeble measures.

He never went back up the ravine, but a year later he found a jumbled pile on the floor of the main canyon. Washed down in a flash flood like so many of the other works of man and God, a clutter of bones and a few patches of leathery white hide. He closed his eyes and imagined what the years ahead would hold: the slow, steady erosion, the sudden pulses of water, the long, baking heat. There was creation and destruction and the inevitable dissolution of all bonds. And he saw how, in the end, everything would travel, as it all must, down to the soft, empty forgetfulness of the sea.

Tim Weed

Six Feet Under the Prairie

Surely I can be forgiven for misjudging Billy Hurley. I was only nineteen that summer, so it's understandable that I didn't see him for more than he appeared at first glance: a thirtyish Okie pretending to be something he wasn't. He couldn't have been a real cowboy anyway, not in this day and age, not even if he did look the part: the sharp-toed shitkickers, the alternating duo of threadbare western-cut shirts, the greasy Custer-length hair, the straw-colored handlebar mustachio of which he was obviously so proud. The crew gave him plenty of guff for this low-budget cowpoke look, but he wasn't easily provoked; he would just shake his head and stare off into the distance, his narrow face taking on an air of moonfaced sadness like a saint in some old Spanish painting.

I'll never forget the day I called him out. I don't know exactly what drove me to it. I was the college boy, summer help, still uneasy among the full-time journeymen on the crew. I suppose I was eager to overcome my discomfort by joining in on the sarcastic workingmen's banter. And though it shames me to think of it now, I must have seen Billy as a safe target.

From afar, the scene would have looked like this: two forest-green utility trucks at rest on a rolling yellow prairie among scattered pine glades and cottonwood gullies; beyond that a band of green foothills; and beyond them the massive blue-dun profile of the Front Range Peaks taking up the western horizon. Close in some and you would smell the air, clean and peppery with sage. Close in some more and you would see five men in hardhats, sprawled out around the trucks in attitudes of insolent relaxation: a line crew on lunch break.

In a surprisingly fluid series of motions Billy whipped off his hardhat, tossed his sandwich into it as he got up, and wiped his hands on his dirty boot-cut Wranglers as he strode over to the utility truck window.

"What'd you call me?"

"A cowboy-wannabe?"

"Step on out here and call me that, you little fuck." His face was only a couple of feet away from mine, and though technically I was bigger, I couldn't help noticing that the tendons under the dry, freckled skin on his neck stood out like leather cords. His eyes—usually vague and bewildered as if he'd gone to sleep by a campfire and woken up by a six-lane highway—had become small and mean, like one of those black-and-white archive photographs of Appalachian dirt farmers. Beyond him, arrayed on the ground and the fenders of the cable truck, were the other journeymen, Bruce, a middle-aged ex-Navy man, and Mike and Ignacio, two Mexican-American cousins in their early thirties. Next to me, in the driver's seat of the utility truck, was Buck Blackshere, the crew chief. I glanced at him for support but he shrugged noncommittally, and I knew I was on my own. I opened the door and slid down off the seat, letting my weight settle onto the soles of my work boots on the hard-packed dirt. It was a cloudless summer day and the sun was hot on my shoulders. I slammed the door of the truck. The sound rolled out over the prairie like a gunshot.

"High Noon," I quipped, my attempt at a smile failing because my throat was all clenched up and I kept needing to swallow. It was the first time I'd seen anyone's temper flare up on the crew. I felt trapped, like a schoolboy who lobs a snowball at a passing car, and the brake-lights go on and the car fishtails to a stop and both doors swing open.

Billy put his head down and came at me. I ducked and grabbed his arm and leaned in—I grew up with an older brother and my reflexes were good for that kind of thing—and he came flying over my shoulder and landed on his backside with his head against the front tire of the truck. I spun to face him, but he just sat there panting in the dust, as if that one lunge had used up all his energy. By now the rest of the crew was having a good laugh at his expense.

My uncle was a Vice President of the Public Service Company of Colorado. He arranged for me to work on a line construction crew that summer, but the idea was my own. I had two years of college behind me, and although this may sound like a cliché, I felt the need for a passage into manhood. Line crews have a reputation for toughness, and a summer of rugged manual labor struck me as exactly the kind of thing I required, like boot camp without the haircut or the long-term commitment.

I was assigned to Buck Blackshere's crew. Buck was probably in his mid-sixties that summer, short and athletically built with a handsome leathery face, silver hair cropped and slicked back like a 1940s film star. He was the kind of chief who inspired his men to work hard without ever raising his voice. I heard him tell jokes and I heard him recite poetry from memory, but I never heard him bark out an order. If you studied his face, as I did, it was possible to detect a certain tiredness—as if he'd seen too much of life—but he kept up a jolly front. It was well known on the crew that in his youth he'd been the state bronc-riding champ for seven years running, and there was an aura of grandeur about him. I could imagine him as the captain of a privateer, or the good-hearted ringleader of a gang of outlaws.

My first morning on the crew coincided with the first day of the crew's main task that summer, to lay down the power grid for the Highlands Ranch project, a big subdivision south of Denver. It was an important job, the vanguard of the suburban development that was pressing southward over the prairie like a fast-growing geometric fungus. Before we left the PSCo warehouse Buck unrolled the blueprints to show us the power grid, a spider-web of pencil lines depicting the network of cables tying together the transformers that would regulate the electricity for each street and cul de sac. When he'd finished going over the plans, he asked if there were any questions. The only one came from Billy Hurley, who asked what type of transformer we'd be installing. Buck read some numbers off the blueprints, and Billy spat tobacco juice into a Coke can and asked about the diameter of the cable. Buck read off a few more numbers and Billy nodded gravely, as if it made a difference. I noticed the other men exchange glances: apparently this was a scenario they'd seen play out before.

The second clash came a few days after the first. It was one of those mornings along the Front Range when the outlines of the mountains are so crisp they could be painted on canvas—a flat backdrop of stone-gray peaks and wide bowls under a pure blue sky. We'd been digging trench, and as we did every day at ten o'clock, we broke for coffee. Preparing the coffee was a grunt's job, so while everyone else relaxed around the utility truck I hoisted myself up and lifted the industrial issue orange-and-white thermos from its bracket and eased it down onto the open door of a side cabinet, which doubled as a work bench. I dropped to the ground and got out a sleeve of Styrofoam coffee cups and stood it on end next to the thermos.

I bowed. "Coffee, your excellencies." Every day I'd been trying out new ways of saying it, using different accents and titles and such, but I had yet to get anyone to crack a smile. Billy usually grimaced, as if the sound of my voice made his ears ring.

"Pour me a cup, pin-dick." He was reclining on a spent cable spool between the truck and the newly dug trench. Everyone's eyes were on me.

"Get it yourself, Billy."

"Bullshit, pin-dick. You get it for me."

I poured a cup, carefully added the non-dairy creamer and a packet of sugar, stirred, and took a sip, all the while staring at Billy, whose lean, freckled face had gone a deep crimson.

"I'm not giving you another chance, college boy. Final warning."

"Knock it off, gentlemen," Buck said mildly. He was looking at a clipboard that he held on his thigh with his elbow, one foot up on the bumper of the truck.

Billy stared at the crew chief and let out his breath in a long whistle, setting the low-drooping sidebars of his moustache trembling like prairie-grass in the wind. Then he steeled himself, and with a kind of full-body shrug he started to get up, but the spool tipped over and pitched him on his backside in the dirt. The big spindle rolled away into the trench as if it wanted nothing to do with the long-haired Okie, and there was a moment of dead silence. Then the whole crew started hooting and snorting.

Billy sat with his legs splayed out on the hard-pack. The sun was getting higher by the minute, and in the heat-shimmer rising up from the ground his scrawny body seemed to quiver and blur, as if it might evaporate or suddenly burst into flame. I kept an eye on him in case he came at me again, but his expression was more sad than angry and he wasn't even looking at me. He was looking at Buck, who was still studying the clipboard, his face hidden in shadow under the brim of his hardhat.

When I was a boy, my grandfather used to take me out to Highlands Ranch to see the West as it used to be. He knew Mr. Carlson, the old rancher, whose family had settled the area along Cherry Creek that would later become Denver way back during the Gold Rush in the mid-1800s. On a good day out at the ranch you could see deer, antelope, coyote, red-tailed hawks, two kinds of falcon, and the occasional golden eagle. There was a horse-path that started from the old stone Victorian mansion and wound along a sandy-bottomed gulch through glades of scrub oak and juniper to the open prairie. After rain the smell of sage was strong in the air, a sharp immaculate wilderness scent that will always be linked in my imagination to Cheyenne hunting parties and buckskin cowboys riding the unfenced plain.

One day—I was probably twelve or thirteen at the time—Grandfather and I came upon a dying calf in a wildflower meadow at the edge of a glade of ponderosas. We heard it before we saw it; it was caught like the prize of some huge, malignant spider in a length of rusted barbed wire, crying out in husky, panicked bleats as it slowly strangled itself. The wire was looped around its neck in such a way that the more it struggled, the tighter the wire became.

"Hold it steady while I try to get it loose," Grandfather said, both of us dismounting. I still remember the fragrant heat of its flanks and the labored heave of its ribcage as I leaned into it and hugged.

Finally we freed it, but its neck was bleeding badly. It tried to stagger away from us but one of its legs was broken or dislocated, and it sank to its knees in the wet buffalo grass, wild-eyed and moaning softly. Grandfather walked over to his horse and unstrapped a .22 rifle from the saddle.

"Do we have to kill it?" I asked.

The old man pursed his lips. He'd been a large-animal veterinarian, and although he was already retired by then, if there was anyone who could do something to save the calf, it was him.

"There must be something we can do," I pleaded.

He put his hand on my shoulder. "All living things must come to their end, Joseph. This calf's time has arrived early, is all."

He held the barrel to the animal's forehead. It stopped moaning and gazed up at us, its sad eyes seeming to comprehend what was in store. I averted my eyes, but the shot rang out and I heard the bullet puncture the animal's skull with a fleshy pop, like cutting into a pumpkin. I turned back in time to see a tremor pass through the calf's body. Then it lay still. We rode back to the mansion in silence, in a light drizzle, with the perfume of sage in our nostrils.

After that Grandfather and I came out to the ranch less often; we would talk about it all the time, but somehow it became harder to arrange. And soon I was a teenager, with plenty of other things on my mind.

Grandfather became ill the summer I worked on Buck's crew. When I visited him in the hospital he asked me what I'd been doing with myself, and when I told him I'd been working out at Highlands Ranch the light came back into his face for a moment. But then he must have realized the nature of the work—falling beef prices and sky-rocketing property taxes had forced the Carlsons to sell out several years earlier—and his eyes dimmed as he let his head sink back into the hospital pillow. I had a strange sensation, as though I was sitting on the edge of a precipice and he was tumbling slowly away from me into the dark void below.

When my mother told me he'd died, the nature of my grief surprised me. It wasn't sadness so much as an overwhelming emptiness, a feeling of loss larger than the hole left by Grandfather's absence. And there was something worrying the edges of that hole, a gnawing sense of guilt that I didn't fully recognize at the time, but that has since grown as familiar as the ache of an ill-fitting pair of boots.

The morning was overcast and gray, a rarity on the Front Range in summer. The mountains were hidden behind a long, dull billow of clouds, and we could have been in Kansas for the featurelessness of the landscape. Bruce and the Mexicans had gone back to the warehouse to load a new spool of cable, and Buck was pacing out the next day's work. I was shoveling out the newly cut bottom of the trench while Billy used the backhoe to open the ground ahead.

I couldn't see the main body of the machine or the man in the cockpit, just the rusted yellow hydraulic arm with its toothed steel bucket as it dipped to scoop a fresh load of dirt, rose and disappeared in the slot of gray sky over the trench, and returned empty a few minutes later.

My job was to square the bottom of the trench so that the cable would lie flat. The dirt was brittle and hard, shot through with rocks ranging from pebbles to boulders the size of anvils; when I came upon one of these bigger rocks I had to use the blade of my shovel to pry it loose. I was concentrating on an especially hard-bitten slab when I felt the trench walls shudder. I straightened, alert to danger, and saw that Billy had let the bucket come to rest, teeth down, on the dirt-pile right above my head. There was a loud hissing in my ears and I remember the cascading dirt giving off a rich metallic odor, like blood.

Then my world went black.

Next thing I knew I was laid out beside the trench, Billy's narrow, wizened face peering into mine. His eyes were inscrutable slits, and the sidebars of his stringy moustache trembled with every breath.

"Cripes, kid, I thought you was a goner for a minute there."

My head throbbed. I seemed to have lost the power of speech.

"Big rock slid off the pile and clobbered you on the head. I climbed down and brung you out." He spat a long stream of tobacco juice, then resumed staring at me. Perhaps it was my imagination, but his voice seemed remarkably calm, and the words sounded artificial, as if he might have been rehearsing them while I was unconscious. I sat up and felt my head; my hair was sticky and full of grit, matted with blood and dirt. In the corner of my eye I saw Buck's compact athletic frame striding briskly toward us with the rolled-up blueprints in one hand. I felt a hot bubble of anger welling up in my esophagus.

"Lads taking coffee break already?" he called good-humoredly, but as he approached he must have sensed something was wrong, because by the time he came up to us his face was stern. "What happened here?"

I glanced up at him and looked away again. "Ask Billy."

The crew chief turned to the wiry journeyman seated on the dirt pile beside me. Billy twitched nervously. "Rock slid off the pile and hit him in the head, Buck. And, ah—he wasn't wearing a hard hat."

Just then Bruce and the Mexicans drove up in the loaded cable truck. Buck helped me to my feet and directed me to the utility truck, where I sat in a kind of daze.

After they'd unloaded the spool I watched Buck take Billy aside to reprimand him. He spoke in a low, even tone and from my vantage point in the truck I couldn't tell what he was saying, but I could see by the way he was jabbing his finger in the air that he was giving the Okie a good dressing down. Billy was shaking his head, and every once in a while he would try to stammer out some kind of defense, but Buck wasn't brooking interruptions. Eventually Billy stopped trying to argue, and his face took on the pale gray shade of poured cement before it sets. The crew chief made a final angry point and Billy spun and stalked over to the backhoe, kicking dirt as he went. He hoisted himself up into the cockpit of the big yellow machine and slouched back in the seat, pulling his hardhat down over his eyes as if he wanted to take a cowboy-style nap out of the sun—only the sun had yet to come out that day.

Buck insisted on a trip downtown to headquarters, though I swore the bump on my head was nothing serious. We took the high road, a dirt track along an elevated ridge with a view of the whole area. Looking out at the landscape, it began to dawn on me that we were really doing a number on the prairie. Old Highlands Ranch was barely recognizable beneath the maze-like ridges of dry, clotted earth piled up along the trenches and foundation holes. I wondered where all the wildlife was going. South probably, although before long the animals would hit Colorado Springs, which was undergoing its own sprawl northward. To the east was farm and feedlot country, where the soil was mostly used up, trampled, eroded away by wind and rain or saturated with chemical fertilizers. All of it had been prairie once. I closed my eyes and imagined rolling hills, herds of buffalo, tall grass swaying in the wind.

We hit pavement on County Line Road and took a right, then veered left at University, which would take us north through the suburbs to downtown Denver. Buck drove in silence, looking wise and rumpled, like an Indian chief with one sculpted brown hand on the wheel and the other resting on a dusty denim-clad knee. Eventually I worked up the nerve to ask him what he'd said to Billy.

"I told him it's his duty to supervise the summer help when the rest of us are gone. And I gave him a few additional tips as well." He glanced in the rearview and said mildly, as if to himself: "I may have been a little hard on the bastard, honestly."

"Did he say how it happened?"

He gave me an angry look. "What are you getting at, kid?"

There was an awkward pause. "Joe," he said after a while, "Hurley may be a fool, and being of your generation, you'd most likely call him a loser. He's got a thin skin, and he lacks the wherewithal to say his piece in such a way that men will shut up and listen. But he ain't deliberately vicious. It was an accident, just like he said." The truck came to a stop at a traffic light and Buck turned to me. "By the way. Don't ever let me hear about you working in a trench without a hard hat on. You got that?"

I felt my ears redden. "I got it."

We drove on in silence. The sun peered shyly through the cloud layer, illuminating a gleam of new snow on the peaks to the west. Nearer at hand, on both sides of the avenue, we drove through a bright panorama of condos and townhouses, unnaturally green lawns with sprinklers going full blast, identical mini-malls of Seven-Elevens and Taco Bells and Kinko's that seemed to be sprouting up throughout the Denver metropolitan area like a vast colony of bright self-cloning mushrooms. We drove into the old suburbs, decaying brick Victorians with drier, weedy lawns, and I reached up to feel my head, the mat of dried blood which for some reason reminded me of Grandfather, who'd died several weeks earlier. In his day these neighborhoods would have been the very outer limits of the city.

"It's a shame," I said aloud, though I didn't mean to say it.

"What's that, Joe?"

I hesitated, embarrassed. "It's a shame what we're doing to the prairie. Back at Highlands Ranch, I mean."

Buck shook his head sadly. "I hear you, kid. But if we weren't doing it someone else would."

I stared out the window, wondering about that. Was my uncle to blame, because he was upper management and we were just worker ants? Or was it the fault of the greedy developers, or, for that matter, of the young middle-class families pursuing their pre-fab version of the American dream? Who could blame them for wanting to watch Rocky Mountain sunsets from their decks?

"I'm sorry about what I implied back there," I said. "About Billy, I mean. I just get the feeling he doesn't like me very much."

"You don't like him very much either, do you?"

"Isn't that a natural reaction to the fact that he doesn't like me?"

Buck regarded me coolly. "It's not as if you really gave him a chance. You called him out, remember? Not the other way around."

I nodded, ears burning. I knew Buck was right, but still . . . I had this sense that Billy had challenged me in some covert way. That he'd somehow put me up to it, and that our little feud was far from over.

The next morning Billy and I were given the job of squaring trench-bottom together. I don't know if it was because of the incident of the day before, or because Buck wanted us to work together, or if he truly felt he needed Billy in the trench; but whatever the reason, the fact that he'd been taken off backhoe duty seemed to bother the Oklahoman quite a bit. It was a hot day, hotter in the trench, where we were exposed to direct sunlight and sheltered from the moderating finger-breezes that came down off the mountains. Billy was using his shovel as a pick to knock off the rough edges left over from the backhoe and I was following behind him, scooping loose dirt and tossing it up onto the bank of the trench.

He'd been absorbed in the work all morning, aggressively silent. Finally he spoke over his shoulder, voice thick with suppressed emotion. "Have a nice ride yesterday?"

"What, down to Medical?" Under my hardhat I felt the slight, almost pleasant ache of the little egg-shaped bump where the rock had hit me. The company doctor had tested for concussion, and there was no cause for concern. "I *did* have a nice ride, thanks, Billy. Thanks to *you*, I mean." I couldn't resist the urge to spar with him, despite what Buck had said. A certain process had been set in motion within me, an automatic attack mechanism that had a life of its own.

"Old Buck tell you some rodeo stories, did he?"

I scooped another shovelful and tossed it up on the bank. "Why, Billy? You jealous?"

He didn't reply, occupying himself instead with a flurry of hard shovel blows at a rock sticking out of the trench wall. I knew he idolized Buck; I believed that it was one of the few things we had in common.

Several minutes passed, then he spoke over his shoulder again. "Everything's easy for you kid, ain't it?"

"What are you talking about?"

He stopped working and turned around, his face red and pinched with anger. "Did you tell him I did it on purpose, you little son of a bitch?"

"No," I replied calmly. "Should I have? I mean, it *was* an accident, wasn't it?" Sweat glistened on my forearms; each little pore was marked with a pinpoint of black dirt. I gripped the shovel handle and braced for a fight.

"Of course it were an *accident*. I just thought you'd tell Buck it weren't."

"What's your problem, Hurley?"

Billy was leaning on his shovel, staring at me.

"Problem? Ain't got no problems. *You're* my only problem, pin-dick." He seemed to have calmed down, but his eyes were unnaturally bright and there was a weird smile playing at the corners of his lips under the drooping moustache. Staring into his face I felt a sensation of vertigo, as if he were exerting some kind of gravitational pull. All of a sudden the walls of the trench seemed to settle and shift inward, and there was that fresh-dirt smell like blood again. Overcome with claustrophobia I dropped my shovel and heaved myself out of the trench, gasping for air. When I was up on the bank I felt a rush of relief, as if I'd just escaped a living burial. Down in the trench Billy shook his head, spat in the dirt, and turned back to the work at hand.

Before I knew it July and half of August had gone by, and it was my final week on the crew. We'd dug twenty miles of trench and outspooled the equivalent length of cable, splicing dozens of army-green transformer boxes into the circuit as we went. The power grid was nearly done; the gas, water, telephone and television crews had laid their PVC pipes and cables, and the homebuilders were excavating and pouring eight to ten foundations a day. Highlands

Ranch looked less and less like the Old West and more and more like what it had become: the largest new housing project in the state of Colorado. My time as an agent of the destruction of that patch of prairie, the landscape of my childhood, was almost at an end. But I'd be lying if I said I was worried about that kind of thing. I was proud of my hardened muscles, basking in the minor triumph of having held my own on a crew of tough working men.

Billy Hurley and I had settled into a kind of détente. Once or twice I'd caught him watching me with a strange intensity, brow furrowed and eyes asquint as if he was trying to puzzle something out; but when I met his gaze he would invariably turn away and spit a stream of tobacco juice in the dirt. He no longer challenged me directly. In fact we rarely spoke at all unless the work required it.

There were lightning storms every afternoon, fast-moving thunderheads gathering over the Front Range peaks and unburdening themselves onto the prairie. Around lunchtime they would form in the high country for their afternoon march downslope, gaining mass as they zigzagged over the foothills and onto the plains surrounding greater Denver. With these storms it was hit or miss. Sometimes they sped away to the east—lightning flashes illuminating the purple clouds like flickering lanterns; the trailing white blur of rain—but when they were on target they hit with violence: rain in roaring sheets, thick multi-forked spars of lightning, earth-rattling thunderclaps and sometimes hail clattering down on the hoods and windshields of the trucks. But the storms' rages were short-lived; the rain broke the heat of the day and left the air fresh and smelling of sage and moist dirt. If nothing else they provided an excuse for me to sit idle in the truck, something Buck insisted on if there was lightning in the area.

On Tuesday August 21—I remember the date exactly—all other details having been attended to, we prepared to make the final splices and bulldoze the dirt into the remaining sections of trench, thus completing the Highlands Ranch power grid and finishing the job. The sky was clear that morning except for a sparse flock of cottonball clouds gathered over the mountaintops, harbingers of the daily pile-up and its afternoon assault upon the plains.

The first surprise was Billy's outfit: he showed up wearing an orange-and-blue Denver Broncos T-shirt instead of his usual western-cut. More strikingly, the mustachio and the stringy Custer-length hair were gone, replaced by a clean shave and a barbershop crewcut. The change did not suit him well. Indeed, he looked very odd, face all out of proportion without the blond tusk-like whiskers, white tan-line halfway up his forehead under the enormous shorn scalp. You would have expected it to fuel a whole week of teasing on the crew, but no one said a word. Apparently none of us felt comfortable joking with him anymore.

Due to the regularity of the thunderstorms, the routine was to take care of any aboveground tasks in the morning and work in the trench in the afternoon; as Buck said, there was no safer place to be with lightning in the air than six feet under the prairie. I was not allowed in the trench, however, when the journeymen were splicing cable. So instead of donning foam rubber safety gloves—the elbow-length orange Day-Glos the men wore to protect themselves against unforeseen power surges—I would simply swing up into the truck to read or play solitaire on the wide vinyl seat.

An hour or so after lunch that day, the thunderheads slid down off the mountains and extinguished the sun, eating back the stunted mid-afternoon shadows and cloaking the dirt piles and trench lines in a weak bluish light. Buck told me to drive the utility truck over to the sector transformer to check on Billy.

"See if he needs anything," he said, reaching into his shirt pocket for a plug of tobacco. "You know which transformer I mean?"

I nodded. It was about a quarter mile off, an army-green box the size of a tipped-over phone booth that held the circuits linking the sector to the rest of the power grid. Under no circumstances, Buck reminded me, was I to go down into the trench with Billy: I was just to see if he needed anything and hand him tools if he asked me to.

I started the truck and followed the ridges of dirt along the trench to the transformer in question. Billy was sitting on top of the box, his foam rubber gloves laid out beside him like slightly flexed amputations, radiating a blurry orange light in the overcast gloom.

I stepped out of the truck. He got up off the box and held out his hand, beaming at me as if we were long-separated *compañeros*. I still couldn't get used to him without the whiskers and the western duds; he looked strangely mischievous, like a spindly, overgrown two-year-old. I took his hand, think-ing that it would be a relief not to have to see him every day now that I was headed back to school.

"That Buck is some kind of thoughtful, ain't he?" he said, keeping hold of my hand in a vice-like squeeze. "Sending my favorite college kid to wait on me hand and foot? Cain't tell you how much I appreciate this. Truly; truly."

"Knock it off, Billy." I jerked my hand out of his grasp and backed away a little. "He told me I was supposed to ask if you needed any help."

He seemed to consider for a moment, and, beaming again, said that there was one simple thing I could do, which would save him the trouble of climb-ing out of the trench. When word came over the radio that it was time to make the splice, he would give me a signal—he would stand up and wave—and at that point I should open the transformer box and flip the power switch to "off."

"Got that, Joey-boy? 'Off,' not 'on.' That's simple enough to remember, what with all that college behind you, eh"—here he attempted the posh British ac-cent I'd used to announce the coffee—"my fine . . . young . . . lad?" He patted me on the shoulder. There was something off-kilter about his voice—the last words had seemed to lag behind the movement of his lips, as in a low-budget foreign movie—and his eyes had retreated inward as if drawn by some cap-tivating private image.

He shook his head and his eyes refocused. He flashed a winning smile and gave me the thumbs-up signal, like a fighter pilot. Then he walked over to the trench and dropped in. I thought about driving back to let Buck know that Billy was acting funny, but if I'd done that I would have risked missing the signal, and it was never my intention to put him in any danger.

The storm broke without warning, a sudden darkening in the air and then the rain was pouring down in sheets. I ran for the truck. From the passenger-side window I had a good view of the spot where Billy had disappeared into the trench, and I kept the window open, despite the soaking the seat was getting, in case he called for me. I figured he was hunkered down, waiting out the worst of the storm.

Then I noticed that his safety gloves were still a bright orange blur on the transformer. Reluctantly, but feeling duty-bound, I got out of the truck, ran over to the transformer to grab the gloves, and continued on to the trench, where he was whittling at the ends of the cables with his utility knife, ignoring the storm raging above.

"Come sit in the truck," I shouted, "until the storm passes!"

"Fuck off," he growled, not looking up from the cables. At that point lightning bolts started hitting nearby—I'd been counting off the ever-shorter delays between the bright forks and the booming thundercracks—and I squatted down to make myself less high-profile, heart pounding in my chest.

"Well at least put these on, for Christ's sake," I yelled, tossing the safety gloves down to him as I turned to sprint, still doubled over, back to the truck. The rain was a torrent drumming the windshield and splattering in through the open window. Every few seconds the lightning illuminated the transformer and the muddy dirt piles, and loud claps of thunder shook the truck and the ground it stood on. I thought about shutting the window and turning on the heat to dry myself off a bit, but I didn't do it, instead keeping a close watch on the trench.

In one of the breaks between thunderclaps I might have heard a faint pop over the drum and sizzle of raindrops, but I can't be sure; there are a lot of noises in a storm and it might have been my imagination. When the rain eased up and the lightning had moved off to a safe distance, I got out of the truck and walked over the slick dirt to the trench. The prairie sage smell was strong, along with the warm mineral pungency of wet earth, but there was something funny mixed in, a sort of chemical tang.

With a dropping feeling in my stomach I paused at the edge of the trench. The first thing I saw was the pair of safety gloves, lying on the trench-bottom where I'd thrown them, palms up as if to catch the raindrops before they dissolved in the mud. Beyond them Billy lay on his side in the fetal position, his pale, hairless face half-submerged in a mud puddle.

My uncle happened to be in the vicinity and heard the radio distress calls, so he got to us first, even before the ambulance. He took me aside and led me over to his car, a white Chrysler with maroon velvet trim, and I sat numbly in the passenger seat while he went to talk to Buck and the other men. They'd already pulled Billy out of the trench and laid him out on the ground beside the cable truck. No one had been able to get his eyes to close, so they stayed open with bits of mud sticking to them like peeled hard-boiled eggs.

The ambulance arrived and its flasher was a hypnotic red pulse inside the Chrysler. I felt numb as the technicians lifted the body onto a stretcher, covered it in a shroud, and loaded it into the ambulance. I could summon no feelings other than relief that my time on the crew was over. I was certain that I would never see any of them again.

My uncle came back and got in the car and I sank into the comfortable seat as he turned the key in the ignition. But there was a tapping at my window, and I looked up to see Buck regarding me through the glass. I straightened in my seat and rolled down the window. His leathery face was close and I could smell the familiar chewing tobacco.

"The only thing I don't understand," he said quietly, "is how the power came to be on when Billy was making the splice."

I felt a spasm of panic down in my crotch. It hadn't really registered that I could be in trouble.

"Well, kid?"

"There was lightning hitting all around. I tried to get him to come sit in the truck, but he wouldn't. I must have missed his signal."

"Signal, Joe? What signal?"

"That's enough," my uncle put in. "Joseph, you don't have to answer any more questions."

"No, it's okay." I swallowed and stared up at Buck. "He said he was going to stand up and wave when he was ready. I was supposed to flip the switch to 'off.'"

"So he had the switch on to begin with?" Buck raised his eyebrows. I nodded. He shook his head slowly. Gray stubble was beginning to show along his jaw-line; suddenly he looked his age. "And he wasn't wearing safety gloves?" he asked quietly.

I would have answered that I'd thrown the gloves down to him, but just then several police cruisers pulled in, blue lights flashing.

"Okay, that's enough." My uncle leaned over to address Buck. "This has nothing to do with my nephew, obviously. I'm taking him home. You can handle it from here, right Blackshere?"

Still gazing at me, Buck gave a single absent nod. There was something in his expression that I'd glimpsed before, a terrible weariness. He tapped the roof of the Chrysler and my uncle drove away. I watched the crew chief in the rearview mirror: the way his shoulders slumped and the effort he had to make to straighten them; how he seemed to take possession of himself then, striding briskly over to the officers and the men gathered by the cable truck. That look in his eyes haunted me. I could detect no warmth for me there, and no forgiveness.

We drove off the site, past the open trenches and the gaping foundation pits for row upon row of new Highlands Ranch homes. I looked west, hoping to find some kind of relief in the soaring peaks, but the Front Range was obscured by clouds. I tried to put myself in Billy's shoes, down in the trench under the dying prairie, with the smell of the mud and the bare wire of the cable ends, with the rain pouring in and the thunder cracking overhead. Would the smell of sage have reached him down there?

Barbara Yost

The Fire Wolves

A lightning strike bore into the earth and Granddad was there to see it happen.

He stubbed out a cigar and pointed to a grove this side of the horizon, not far from the cabin.

"They'll come now," he said. "You watch. It starts with just a few, yapping and chasing their tails, but their pack will grow until there are hundreds, then thousands, and it won't stop without a fight. We're in for it, I'm afraid."

Marilyn came to the porch. "Where are they, Pop?"

"Look to that stand of piñons. It's just a puff of smoke that comes out of their nostrils. In a little while we'll see the coals glowing in their eyes. It's their eyes that ignite the blaze and their breath that fans the flames."

"How much time do we have?" She stared at the white puffs that looked as harmless as cotton threads.

"Two days maybe. It depends on the wind. They race with the wind, you know. If the breeze blows this way, they'll come running and swallow everything in their path. They're a hungry bunch who'll eat their weight before they're through. Ponderosas, piñons, lodgepoles, junipers, but mostly they're hungry for scrub, brush, and chaparral. They're lazy, these fire wolves, and the brush goes down easy. The more they eat, the faster they run, the bigger they grow, the more they eat. No harm in packing things up and being ready if they come this way. They'll devour us, too."

Black billows rose where the white puffs had been.

Tug pulled the truck close to the cabin. He gave Ben a box.

"Put your things in here, boy. Whatever fits, goes."

Ben knelt to a scruff of a white dog with straight-up ears and eyes that looked bigger ringed with tearstains. "Stay put, Champ. This is no time to run off. You stick close by." He ruffled the pup's head.

Marilyn opened the closet and the pantry. Life went into a 20 by 20 carton. Two albums of photographs. Blue baby shoes. Pink love letters. Tackle box. Safe deposit box keys. videocasette marked "Wedding," whose wedding not identified but known. Music box. Box of cigars. Matches. Boxes of macaroni and cheese. Canned tuna with a pop top. Powdered milk, mostly used in winter when the cabin was snowed in. One flashlight and another. Stacks of T-shirts and blue jeans in four sizes and two genders. In the boy's, a brown leather leash, rawhide bone, baseball and glove, magnifying glass, Army men, fishing reel, Potter book, letter from the governor for perfect attendance, jar of peanut butter because it was a necessity.

Whose life fits into one small box?

Champ wore an orange Ripstop vest. His collar and tags were put in place and tightened. Eyes wiped. Pads oiled.

Marilyn dusted and ran the vacuum, washed dishes and wiped down the countertops until they gleamed. She folded linen towels and hung them from the handle of the oven. Brushed crumbs from the breadbox. Threw away a sliver of soap. Polished the faucet. Shook out the placemats. Scoured the sink.

"If the fire comes through, this will all be ash," Tug reminded her, not unkindly.

"Might as well look clean before," she told him and took the vacuum hose to the curtains. "There's food in the refrigerator. It'll be rotted when we get back."

"We'll have a feast before we leave. The freezer might make it. Or maybe the fire wolves will eat through it."

"That'll be their feast."

"I'd like to put rat poison in there."

"They're just following Mother Nature, can't help their nature. There's all that brush out there."

"They kill."

"We make it easy."

For hours, Granddad sat on the porch in an Adirondack chair savoring a cigar. The wolf pack was growing, a black menace with eyes burning red, maws devouring underbrush and scrub. They slid on their bellies between the trees and licked at the beetle-bared bark, dared to climb the piñons and the ponderosas and the junipers with claws that shredded the trunks. They ate what they shredded and licked their chops. They climbed high and stretched above the topmost branches inflamed yellow and orange and red, their tongues ten feet long tasting destruction, and it tasted like victory over the forest. Only char was left behind. They snapped their massive jaws at each other and fought over limbs, swallowing some whole, spitting out dust.

They washed the dust from their throats by guzzling the blood of mice and rabbits and squirrels and voles. Foolish badgers and raccoons could not run fast enough and disappeared into the belly of the beasts. The beasts tried for the mule deer, but the fleet-footed deer scampered and darted, evaded the fire wolves. A cougar fell. The fire wolves picked their teeth with his bones.

Hawks and goldfinches and ash-throated flycatchers caught thermals created by the heat of the flames and rose through the air above the inferno but singed their feathers and breathed in ash. Some escaped. The hawks beat their wings against coarse paws that reached for them and flew to the cool refuge of Lynx Lake. The finches and flycatchers succumbed and no one was there to grieve. Moths and yellow cloudless sulphurs told themselves to be brave, but their delicate wings were no match for the dragon breath of the fire wolves who caught them on their tongues like snowflakes, relished the delicacy, and went looking for more.

The more they ate, the more they craved. Now a great spread lay before them, a banquet, a feast.

"How much longer, Granddad?" Ben sat in a chair his size on the porch next to the box that held eight years of a boy's life.

"We might have a few days," the old man said, "but they're coming fast as the apocalypse."

It was not the first time Walter McKee had watched the fire wolves coming. Twice before, he'd seen the pack. Once, he was Ben's age and had such a box as the boy had now, packed with marbles and comic books and trinkets of boyhood, a nugget of fool's gold, a bag of copper ore, a petrified rat. The fire wolves had spared his family but taken his house as their due, feasted on walls and carpets and pine log furniture, bed posts, knotty pine cabinets, his mother's chintz curtains, her hand-stitched quilts, an abandoned wedding dress. They had left with full bellies, appetites satiated.

Until the next time. The fire wolves came again when Granddad had a wife named Emma and Marilyn was nine. They fled with their boxes as the fire wolves ran up the front steps nipping at the heels of the fleeing McKees but missed the taste of flesh until Emma dropped her box and ran back inside before Walter could grab her arm. She fell to the fire wolves who found her sweet and tender but only a morsel, really. Their dragon breath drove Walter and Marilyn back, back, away from the forest for two days until the cinders settled and the smoldering timbers cooled. Her body lay in repose, blackened, fetal, the bones of her fist curled around a twist of silver, once a baby rattle, only the MAR L N still etched there. She was buried with it, and that gave Walter some comfort. But he never forgot the smell of the burning hide of the fire wolves. He regretted that he did not die lying next to Emma, that the pack had chased him away. But Marilyn was saved. The next time the fire wolves came, Marilyn was all he would put into his box because nothing else mattered.

Now the pack was coming again. Already he could smell the heat of their fur, though they were still miles away, running at the speed of sorrow. Their bellies would already be bloated, full of wood and flesh, forest and homes, automobiles, bicycles, birds and mammals, their canines stained red. Slurry dropped from above, but they drank it down. A little rain came, but it sputtered and turned to steam. Men chopped at their path, cleared away the brush that fed them, beat back flames, and some gave their lives as they fell to the fire wolves.

And the beasts raced on.

For three days, the gorging continued unabated.

"I've got the boxes packed in the truck, Pop," Tug told him. "I guess we'll know in the morning what time to head out. Radio says the shelters have vacancies. We'll have beds and food. We'll be safe. It's already at 2,000 acres, 20 percent containment. The wind should die down tonight, pick up tomorrow."

Granddad put a pair of binoculars to his face, twisted them into focus.

"They're hungry and not yet half full. They started out scrawny, rib bones sticking out over empty bellies, and they went looking for food. When they found it, they got bold." He swept one arm along the landscape. "Look there, black as far as the eye can see from the scrub on the floor to the tops of the ponderosas. We should have been feeding them bit by bit all along, appeasing their appetites just enough to keep them at bay. But we slacked off and made it easy for them. We should have cleared the scrub, but we put out the feed bag, let the loggers have their way."

Tug put his phone back in his pocket. "They got the Ashcraft cabin and Conrad's place, and there's two fatalities so far, eaten down to the bone. You pack your box? I saved a spot in the truck for whatever you want to bring."

Granddad watched an elk sprint away from the inferno, yellow eyes wide with fear, stumbling as he ran, but he caught himself and got away. His tail was gone, his back legs dusted with soot where the fire wolves had brushed by and left their mark.

The boy came outside to witness the pack advancing. He sat on the porch with his legs crossed, dog following.

"I don't smell anything," Ben said, nervously socking a baseball into a glove over and over.

"The wind's blowing their scent away from us," Granddad said. "When we smell them, it's time to go."

"They look so close."

"Not so close, boy," Tug said. "We won't let them get close. Don't you worry."

"But what about Grandma? They got close to her. They got her. The big bad fire wolves ate her."

Granddad put his hand on the boy's head. "She had a mission. Your mission is to get away. You've got your box. You don't need to get close."

Champ gave a whimper and took to Ben's lap. Ben put down his glove and scratched the dog's ears. "I'll keep you safe, Champ. The fire wolves won't get you. I promise."

Emma was on Marilyn's mind as she brought out coffee, milk for the boy. If she tried hard, she could conjure an image of her mother, but it was years old and fading like drapes bleached in the sun. When the fire wolves came for the McKees, she had turned her head once and saw her mother run into the cabin, felt her father reach in vain and then drag his girl away as she screamed and tried to pull back, dropped her own box and left everything behind. She lost the thing she cared for most for the sake of a silver rattle.

Marilyn grew up fierce and protective of those around her. For the last three days, she had kept Ben in her sights. If he wandered, she screamed herself hoarse. Tug had wanted to drive to the fire and get a better look. She threatened divorce. Her father stayed on the porch, knowing the rebuke that would come if he strayed. Not only Champ was on a leash. Marilyn held tight.

A telephone rang inside. Marilyn walked out talking. "Fine, then." She flipped it closed. "Mandatory evacuation tomorrow. They'll let us know when."

"We'll know when," Granddad said.

"You pack your box, Pop? Your blood pressure medication? Your wallet? Medicare card? Your journals? That cap from New York City? I can get you a bag if that's easier, or a valise."

A column rose up five miles away between the piñons and the junipers. Hundreds of fire wolves climbed on top of each other like voracious acrobats to devour the tops of the pines, swayed in the updrafts, and surveyed what lay ahead of the omnivores. More piñons and junipers, a meal of lodgepole pines. Wild turkeys, doves, quail, and band-tailed pigeons were already roasting in the underbrush. The fire wolves smelled a banquet and tucked in their napkins.

"You pack your box, Pop, or I'll pack it for you."

Ben leaned into Granddad's ear. "You'd better do it. Mom doesn't take no for an answer."

"No one knows that better than I do."

The phone again. Ashcrofts were at the shelter. Conrad had his family there. Lopez, Carter, Parker families were packing up. The Red Cross was bringing food boxes. Restaurants were donating goods that would spoil in their refrigerators and walk-in freezers and likely to melt if immolated. Volunteers lined up to serve. Help came from all over.

"We're ready," Tug told his family.

A state trooper's car came up the road to the cabin. The officer tipped his hat.

"You'll have to evacuate tomorrow, folks," he said. "If the wind shifts, they'll run this way. They'll take the cabin and anybody in it. We're working around the clock, but they're beasts and we can't beat them back fast enough."

Tug nodded at the truck. "We're packed up, officer. Nothing's worth risking our lives at this point. We're clearing out in the morning as soon as we see which way the wind blows."

Marilyn said, "Of course we're hoping it blows the other way. Sometimes it does and they run with it. We built this place ourselves. It would be nice to hold on to it."

The trooper tipped his hat again and went to his car. "You hope all you want, ma'am, but you be ready to evacuate. Nothing's worth risking your lives. Cabins can be rebuilt."

Granddad sniffed the air. He lit a cigar and took a long draft.

Their last supper in the cabin was eclectic. Meatball sandwiches, corn chips. Fruit was sparse but everyone got a few pieces. Celery, limp lettuce, tomatoes ready to turn, hamburger still fresh for more sandwiches, potato salad from the Fourth of July not yet spoiled, a chocolate cake that wasn't going to survive the fire wolves.

Ben dug in. "This is the best dinner ever," he said, assured that it was wise to have three pieces of cake rather than waste it. To the boy with a glove and a dog, it was an adventure and they were all immortal. Nothing, not even the ravenous fire wolves, could harm them.

Champ got more scraps than he had seen in his short lifetime and the feast calmed his nerves. It gave him gas, but he stretched out on the tile floor and sighed in contentment, licking crumbs from his muzzle, cleaning his face with a paw.

Marilyn dropped a carton on the countertop. "I packed your box, Pop. Tug will put it in the truck. You're set to go."

Granddad took a second piece of cake.

"I built this house a year after your mother died. I was going to duplicate it exactly, I still had the plans, but I was afraid the ghosts would haunt me. So the floor plan is different. It's made of different wood. I put in two and a half bathrooms instead of one. The square footage doubled. The porch is larger. Countertops are soapstone instead of tile. Cabinets are whitewashed oak. It's a completely different house, one that Emma would never recognize. But somehow she found her way back here. Sometimes I hear her singing in the morning. I can smell her perfume. The air stirs and I feel her hand on my face. Sometimes I even hear that silver rattle."

They ate in silence then. Maybe Marilyn heard a soft voice or remembered the outline of a face. She cleared the table, scrubbed down the soapstone and wiped the oak cabinets Tug had whitewashed. She smoothed the curtains she had made, straightened the rugs she had hooked. Tug took the garbage out back. When Champ whined, Ben walked him on a leash to do his business in a bed of pine needles.

Before the sun set, Tug took a hoe and shovel and finished digging a trench around the cabin like a moat around a castle. Granddad and Ben raked dry brush and needles and carried them far from the house.

"Not much more we can do," Tug said with a shrug that Granddad returned.

"Not much, son. Put your shovel away now."

After the sun went down, they sunk into Adirondacks and watched the glow of the fire wolves performing their furious dance, running rings around the pines and tossing themselves into the air with licks of yellow and orange and red that backlit the remaining trees shivering at their fate. If trees had legs, they would have run. They stood as easy prey. Mice and grey squirrels scampered up their trunks for shelter only to lose their fur, then their flesh, and then their beating hearts.

"Turn in," Tug said. "We'll be up early."

If any of the family slept, they did not remember. They listened to the crews fighting the fire wolves, the fire wolves baying at the full moon and sucking mouse flesh out of their teeth. Owls screeched fleeing their nests. Granddad sniffed the air through open windows for the scent of singed fur and charred pines that would mean the wind had shifted. It still might blow the other way, and that would save the house Walter McKee had built.

The wind could be as willful as the wolves.

Sunrise mimicked sunset. Blackened trees stood pitifully against yellow and orange and red glowing a mile away. The fire wolves had grown huge, their pack galloping across 3,000 acres, gluttonous in their pursuit of trees and the odd home, even boulders, two more bodies left behind like dry leaves.

Marilyn woke to find her father standing on the porch, shaking his head at the mischief of the fire wolves. Tug came with a cup of coffee and a donut.

The air was still as a tomb and then the breeze they had been listening for came whistling with a vengeance and for the first time they smelled burning wood and ash and smoldering pine and the roasting flesh of small animals and that smell said everything had shifted. In kind, the fire wolves would shift course and trail their own scent.

"Damn," Tug said.

Snowflakes of ash came from the sky. For Tug and Walter, the fire wolves no longer afforded a clear view but did their evil business behind a curtain of smoke. In the doorway, Ben coughed twice.

"Time to go," Granddad said.

They dressed in minutes and took last-minute provisions. A box of cookies. A second Potter book. A pearl bracelet.

Tug tucked his family into the truck, Marilyn in front, Ben and Champ in back.

"You're in back there with Ben," he told Walter. "I put in your lumbar cushion. Don't mind the dog."

Granddad was sitting in his Adirondack with the look of permanence.

"Glad to see it," he said. "You all run along now before the smoke gets choky."

Marilyn bolted from the truck and screamed at her father where he sat in his chair. "What in hell are you saying? You get in the truck right now, or we're not leaving. You're a crazy old man. You can't stay here. You heard what the trooper said. The fire wolves will devour the cabin and you with it. I won't lose another parent to those creatures."

Granddad lit a cigar. "I'm 80. I can go any time. Emma's here, can't you hear her? I know how you feel, Mari, but I won't leave her again. Yes, I'd rather die. Let me kiss you good-bye and then you be off. The smoke is getting strong. The fire wolves are pounding the earth. I can feel the vibrations."

Marilyn turned to Tug.

He jumped up the steps to the porch. "We won't leave without you, Walter. And then we'll all die. You, me, Marilyn, Ben, and Champ. They'll find our charred bodies and the whole town will mourn. Don't do this. You come on now. Emma will come with us."

Granddad shook his head. "No, she won't leave here. She can't, don't you know? This is her home, too. She's telling me to go, but I guess I'd just rather stay. Now you go on."

Marilyn took out a handkerchief and put it over her nose. "We can't breathe here. It will be a terrible death. We'll suffocate and then we'll burn to death. Pop, you have to come." She sobbed with her mouth open gasping for breath.

Walter pulled her close and took both her hands. The white handkerchief fell from her fingers. It was black with ash. He kissed her cheek and then the other one.

"I've had a good life for the most part. I'm ready to go. Please do this for me. I've got to be where my Emma is. I lost her once. I won't lose her again. I know you wouldn't leave Tug." He released her hands.

Paralyzed, she needed help walking to the truck. Her eyes were vacant, her sobs hanging somewhere in the smoke and the ash. She stared at her father as they headed down the path for the shelter. Granddad did not meet her eyes as she took her last look. Mercifully she fainted at the fork in the road. The truck headed down one path toward safety as the fire wolves galloped down the other.

Two days passed before fire marshals and troopers announced the evacuation order had been lifted. A hundred times a day, Marilyn telephoned the cabin, but the lines were long dead. She might have been a corpse, so little life remained in her body. Ben and Champ took comfort in each other. They ate the food the Red Cross provided. Tug picked at his. Marilyn couldn't look at it and said the sight made her sick. Tug held her and stroked her head and tried a hundred times a day to get her to eat, no use. A hundred times a day she vomited and nothing was there.

Sally Ashcroft came by and talked softly to her. Angela Lopez held her when Tug went outside to breathe fresh air finally cleansed of smoke. Ben brought Champ to be at her side. The dog licked her hand over and over until she put skeletal fingers on his downy head and stroked without feeling.

On the afternoon of the second day, the trooper came by where the family sat on a cot. He tipped his hat. "You're free to go home, folks."

Tug looked around. His family was the only one left at the shelter. The Red Cross was taking away bags of trash and uneaten food and dog chow no longer needed. They had packed up bottled water and paper slippers and daily newspapers. The trooper tipped his hat as the last volunteer closed the door behind her.

Tug hugged his wife. "Let's go home."

"We don't have one."

"Let's see what can be salvaged. If it's gone, we'll drive to Prescott and stay with Aunt Jane."

"I can't go home."

"Please, Mom," Ben said. "We have to go. It will be all right." In two days, he had grown fierce and protective. In two days, he had grown up.

The road back was littered with blackened tree limbs and pieces of axe handle, burned chain saws, melted water bottles little more than lumps of plastic. Granite boulders scattered across the landscape had split open from the heat. It was all a black and white photograph where once color had painted the leaves and the wildflowers.

Charred spikes that once proudly called themselves trees sparsely dotted what once was called forest. Some timbers stood, some fell crosswise. The land underneath was clear, barren. Without fuel, no fire would burn here for many years. But topped of their stems, many plants would be stimulated to sink roots again. Pinecones burst open in the fire would drop seeds and germinate. Roots of ponderosas run deep and those that survived the jaws of the fire wolves would regenerate. Lodgepole pine seedlings could return in two or three years. The forest would come back. Ashes to ashes, and then rebirth.

An elk without a tail crossed their path and ran for cover, finding none, not yet.

Marilyn slumped against the door of the truck. Nothing they passed caught her eye. No bump in the road jarred her. Tug stared straight ahead and mourned for his wife as Walter mourned for his. Ben buried his face against Champ frightened for his mother and frightened of what they would see when they reached home. Their house would be gone. Granddad was gone. Ben had a baseball, a glove, and a dog.

Tug had to drive around fallen limbs and dodged a boulder rolled into the roadway. Another bend, and their cabin would come into view. Unwittingly, he slowed.

"Just get there," the dead voice demanded.

Tug gunned the truck.

Trees and scrub around the house, beyond the trench he had dug, were lifeless gray and black. Chunks of wood lay in piles like lumps of coal in a naughty child's stocking. Earth like coal dust. Ash like gray snow.

Marilyn sat up and looked at her home. The side was scorched. The roof sagged at that spot. For the rest, the cabin stood strong. Porch posts were covered in soot, but the porch itself was sound. The Adirondacks stood sentinel on the side away from the char, in need of dusting. They might have been waiting for spring cleaning.

"You go in," she told Tug. "Ben, stay here."

Tug's eyes looked heavenward for a moment, and then he turned off the ignition and got out of the truck, his boots slipping a little on an ash pile. He grabbed the door handle to steady himself. His foot tested the porch stairs and he heard a good solid thud, went up the steps and stood at the front door that was cracked open a little. He heard a gasp from the truck. The door creaked as it opened, and he went inside. The interior was intact for the most part, though a sliver of sunlight came through the side where the roof sagged. Two inches of ash had blown across everything in the living room and the kitchen. The curtains hung gray. The sink so recently polished was filthy. He'd warned her, hadn't he? The soapstone thick with grit.

"Pop?" Tug called softly. "Are you here? Walter?"

A great-horned owl hooted over the space in the roof.

Tug looked into the bathroom and his heart stopped as he pushed open the door of Walter's bedroom. The handmade quilt that had been yellow and grass green was creased black and gray. Pillows once pristine might have come up from the ground so covered in dirt were they now.

"Granddad?"

The bed was empty, neatly made.

Tug walked back out the front door and shrugged at Marilyn who was pressed against the window, her mouth open in a silent cry, her nails scratching at the glass.

Ben yanked open his door and he and Champ tumbled out.

"Granddad! Granddad! We're home! Where are you?"

He and the dog raced around the house, went into the storage shed that had survived, called and shouted and barked. The owl flew away. One of its tufts was missing.

Marilyn eased herself out of the truck and walked on wobbly legs up to the porch. She put her hand to her eyes and looked across the landscape, looking for footprints in the ash or a body covered over. Something that looked like Pompeii.

"Pop!" she said as her voice found its scream. A grey squirrel scurried away, frightened by the sudden return of other animals. "Pop!"

She fell against the porch railing, fingers making streaks in the soot. Tug came to her. Together they listened for the most meager of sounds, even the whine of a ghost.

"Hey, Champ," Ben said.

The dog's ears twitched. He spun in circles, and Marilyn thought he had gone mad, and then he darted off, barking and bouncing as he skidded in the ash. He fell and got up, white dog turned gray, and raced on.

"Come back, Champ!" Ben called and started to run.

"Stay here, Ben," Tug shouted and reached for his boy but the boy slipped free, unafraid. "It might be one more fire wolf, smoldering, ready to ignite again. Champ will come back. Let him go."

Champ did come back and he was not alone.

Granddad was limping. He was shaking out his hair, dripping water to his chin. Clothes soaked. Beard grizzled.

He winced in pain as Marilyn threw herself against him and forced weight on a bad ankle.

"I twisted it coming down the porch steps," he said as he pressed her to his chest and ran a wet hand over her hair, held out another to shake Tug's, then stroked Ben's head and also touched a paw that pressed against his leg, contacting every inch of his family.

Marilyn could not let go so they walked as one up to the porch and took to their chairs, little caring for the soot they sunk into. She looked to Granddad for an explanation.

"They were monsters," he said, wiping water from his face. "They came at me with a fury, must have been a thousand of them, with their eyes glowing and their fur slick with flames, jaws snapping, feet pounding the ground like thunder. I sat in my chair and I could feel Emma's hand take mine. It was young and soft. The wind whipped like a banshee, but I hung on to Emma and she clung to me and we closed our eyes against the ash that bit into our faces. She squeezed my hand and it felt fierce. I could almost see her body as the ash gave her a gray silhouette. And then the wind changed again as suddenly as before, and the pack only brushed the side of the house. When it was so hot we thought we'd melt, Emma and I ran for the pond and waited until the fire wolves had passed by. As they hit the firebreak, they howled and fell dead and were swallowed by the earth."

"It's all contained now," Tug said. "We can rebuild the cabin."

Granddad fished a cigar from his pocket but it was soaked. The cabin shook itself, the way Champ did, and some of the ash snowed down. "Yep, not so much damage. I did it once, I can do it again."

Marilyn leaned close and whispered, "Is mother still here?"

"No, dear. She's gone now. But this time I got to say good-bye."

NON-FICTION

Harrison Candelaria Fletcher

Prayer For Rain

Rescuing, my mother calls it. Gathering artifacts from the roadside weeds and red desert sand. Nails. Roots. Barbed wire. Bones. She carries them to her home and breathes them alive with story, memory, and dream.

She does not know what she seeks. She does not know if she will return with full pockets. She ventures into the badlands with only a prayer to St. Anthony and a belief: If she is meant to find something, she will.

Trust in this, she tells me. And it will happen.

Heat rises from the badlands highway west of Albuquerque, pooling between hills like liquid silver, or mirrors of air. Ahead on the horizon, thunderheads boil. My uncle raises a finger from the wheel and in his Sunday sermon baritone, says, "Really coming down. And just where we're headed." In the back seat my mother smooths her salt-cedar hair. "Jesus, Mary and Joseph. Take this storm from our path." It's mid-morning. Late summer. Our journey has just begun.

I settle in riding shotgun, and stare into the vanishing point of Interstate 40 and Mesa Chivato, conjuring an image of our destination—Marquez, mythic Marquez, the yellow stone village where my grandfather Carlos found sanctuary after running away from a boarding school in Santa Fe. I heard the story often growing up, so often it has become my own, shimmering as bright inside me as if I walked the hot sand myself. Decades from my New Mexican roots, with a wife, children and life my own, I have come to renew my connection to that place and time, to ground myself in my mother's words, but I'm not sure if that feeling remains, if the village exists, or if it's all a mirage.

We're not prepared for this trip. Not really. My uncle, my mother's youngest brother, a newly ordained priest, has taken a day off from his parish near Taos to be our driver. He wears black slacks, black crew neck, black work shoes, the image of Al Pacino, even in middle age. My mother, third oldest of eight, wears her usual denim housedress, straw sunhat and Jackie O sunglasses, cheeks flushed with anticipation, strength finally returning eighteen months after open-heart surgery. Me, I'm even more out of place in cargo shorts, Denver Nuggets T-shirt, cross trainers. We have no canteens. No compass. No map. We travel, as we have since I was a boy, on instinct, curiosity, faith.

"Looks bad," I say, squinting at the smoky clouds. "Maybe we should turn back."

"Why?" My uncle scowls. "We can make it."

He glances at my mother, who makes the sign of the cross, then he reaches toward the rearview mirror and caresses a strand of pale blue rosary beads.

Carlos. Wayward Carlos. Forever called to the road. The oldest of five children, he was born to a farmer in Puerto del Luna, one hundred miles west of the Texas border. When his father died from a fever his mother married a rancher who refused to raise another man's son, and sent Carlos to the nuns in Santa Fe. He ran away whenever he could, stealing a horse, hitching a ride, but despite his mother's pleas, was never allowed home. From a fencepost he watched his family sit down for dinner, reflection fading in the window glass.

In Marquez, villagers accepted him as one of their own, as one of the hired hands that blew through the mountains on their way from Grants to Albuquerque. He worked odd jobs, made a few friends, slept in a shallow cave fitted with a potbelly stove and a painted wall of angels and saints. For a few seasons, in the embrace of those yellow hills before hitching a boxcar to Denver, Chicago and beyond, Carlos found what he had lost, what had been taken from him, and he never forgot.

My mother didn't, either. She visited Marquez often when I was a boy, standing beside Carlos while his hands took flight with story, drinking in his words. Too young to understand, I collected pebbles with my four siblings, slid down the smooth volcanic flows above the village, and gazed at the woman on the cave wall dressed in blue, arms open, waiting.

* * *

We turn north at Laguna Pueblo onto a narrow gravel road winding toward Marquez like an endless rope, pulling us past Paguate, Seyboyeta, Moquino, village names I've never heard of before, village names that stick on my tongue, tart as cactus candy, when I try to say them aloud. Behind us, the vanishing shapes of semi-trucks, filling stations and reservation casinos lining Interstate 40. Drowsy from the heat, we stare through open windows at the vast buckskin plains speckled with gray tufts of chamisal, yellow splashes of range grass, mossy sprigs of piñon. The farther we drive, the sharper the colors become, the more pronounced the contrasts, white sand against obsidian shadows, yellow daisies sprouting from driftwood, every blade, every branch, bent, twisted, reaching toward water and shade, shaped by this unforgiving land, yet somehow enduring. In a swirl of dust I see the khaki silhouette of my adolescent grandfather straggling over the charred gristle escarpment, lanky, sunburned, an apparition of rags pushing through hell toward a liquid vision of home. I feel that pull myself, firm ground, blue shade, a resting place.

"It's a wonder he survived," I hear myself saying. "Out here. In this."

My mother touches my shoulder. "His friend knew the way. He was from Marquez, but stayed in Santa Fe during the off-season to learn how to read and write. Ranchers did that a lot in those days—sent kids to boarding school. His friend got homesick and took Granddad with him."

My uncle nods. "They made it all that way. By themselves."

"But how?" I ask. "A hundred and fifty miles? On foot?"

"They followed the Rio Puerco as long as they could, then turned west toward Mount Taylor," my mother says. "They ate the jerky and cheese they brought. Picked apples and piñon. Slept in barns and shepherd's shacks during the heat of the day, then traveled at night. They lived off the land like they had been taught. Like they had all their lives. Don't you believe me?"

I tell her that I do—always have—but seeing the land now it doesn't seem possible.

"It was a miracle," she says, and withdraws her hand.

We drive in silence. Gravel pops beneath the tires. Dust swirls through the air.

My uncle steers past a hillside of stones as white as chalk. Under the bare-bulb sun, a shape takes form on the summit—a shack, square as a helmet, leaning forward from its pale camouflage. Through the empty windows, I see two rectangles of turquoise sky.

"He probably stayed there," my mother says, pinching my arm. "Told you it was true."

I explain that I never doubted her, that I only want to see more clearly, but she withdraws.

A few miles from the shack, we pass what first appears to be an arroyo, but as we pull closer, becomes a ravine, then a canyon, 100 feet deep, as if the ground split open during an earthquake.

We park and scramble outside. My mother grips my shoulder as I approach the edge.

"Not too close. There are sinkholes all around. You could fall in."

"She's right," my uncle says, scanning the ground. "Looks can be deceiving."

I stare into the canyon, trying to find the water, the spring keeping this land alive, but I can make out only a flicker, a shadow, there and gone, just out of sight.

Thunder rumbles. We scramble to the car, and leave.

Approaching the blue Stetson of Mount Taylor, the landscape changes again—from yellow brown to chalky white, as if the grass has been dusted with ash. Boulders scatter the hills.

My mother reaches over from the back seat to touch my uncle's shoulder. "Remember my horseshoe? Aren't we close to where I found it? By those rocks?"

Nodding, he points over the dashboard toward a small pile of stones just off the shoulder to our right, a few dozen yards east. "Good memory. Right up there. A little farther ahead."

A year earlier, the two of them had visited Marquez for the first time in nearly a decade. Instead of traveling in the summer heat as they usually did, they drove in the early spring to see the daisies and asters blooming white and purple among the waves of buffalo grass and sage. Creeping along the gravel road, my mother noticed a thin black shape twisting up through the stones.

My uncle parked on the roadside. The shape wasn't moving, so they stepped outside, wary of stirring diamondbacks from hibernation. As she approached, my mother slipped off her bifocals.

"It's not a snake. It's a piece of metal."

She pulled free a rusty horseshoe bent into an "S." Turning it over, she discovered an engraved name and date she recognized from one of her father's stories, a family that had taken him in: "Enselmo Marquez." The relic had been kicked off by a horse, they guessed, or had been left as a marking for travelers. Whatever it was, my mother took it as a sign that she was meant to return.

Our car slows on the shoulder. I squint at the hillside, believing completely her connection to land and spirit, but as I try to will my own vision into shape, I see only dust and shadow.

"Don't know how she saw it," my uncle says, laughing. "With all that rock and cactus? And with her eyesight? It was a miracle."

"Yes," my mother says, eyes wide. "For some reason I was meant to find it."

My uncle hits the brakes. "There! Right there."

I follow his line of sight toward a small pyramid of stones stacked against the face of a white boulder. Instead of a horseshoe, I spot a name painted in black: "ENSELMO MARQUEZ, '22."

My uncle nods. My mother makes the sign of a cross.

"Quite a coincidence," I say, slipping off my sunglasses.

"No," my mother says. "He must have died there. His family wanted us to see him. To pray for him. There are restless souls all around."

My uncle whispers a prayer. My mother lowers her head. I stare at the name, shimmering in the heat—liquid, edged in silver, alive.

The road angles east, away from the storm. We climb a steep hillside surrounded by cedar and pine. Descending into a valley, my uncle leans back. "There it is. Marquez."

Straight across from us on the opposite side of a deep, jagged arroyo stands two dozen stone houses scattered on the mesa like toy blocks, the rusty tin roofs and yellow-brown walls blending in perfectly with the rattlesnake skin of the landscape. Most of the homes have crumbled into the brush, but among the ruins, I see the white propane tanks and utility lines of the remaining inhabitants.

My mother touches my arm. "We made it."

I look around to orient myself to his place, to my memory of it, left toward the rocky yellow hills, right toward stands of cedar and pine, but I don't recognize a thing.

"Where's the cave?"

My uncle points to an outcrop of pink boulders to my right.

"By that formation."

I roll down my window for a clearer view. Between the pine branches, I see a wall of smooth sandstone sloping down the hillside like the folds of a cloak. Bellow it, the black mouth of a cave.

A memory: Sliding on my Keds down the slick rock pretending to be a Conquistador searching for lost gold. Carlos stands below me at the cave opening, fedora tipped back, smiling, speaking in Spanish to my mother, who stares through her Jackie-O's at the shapes inside.

"Think the cave's still there?" I ask, holding tight to those images, which only become more important to me the farther removed from New Mexico I become.

"One way to find out."

My uncle flicks off the ignition and steps outside. My mother snatches her sun hat and follows. I hike a dozen yards ahead, cutting across a ravine just south of the car, still trying to match the landscape before me to the landscape of my imagination. In the distance, I hear their voices.

"Look at this. An arrowhead!"

"And here. Another one."

Grinning at the echoes of my childhood, I scour the ground myself, marveling at how every stone and root is more vivid under the naked sun, as if I've awakened from a dream, or rather, touching ground I was not sure existed, but see now as real. A strange rock catches my eye: yellow with a scarlet mineral deposit twisting through the center like an artery. Turning it in my fingers, I see a living thing with its own story and past, like the artifacts in my mother's home, waiting to awaken with a touch. Next I pause before a choya twisted into a cross, or a crucifix, another living memorial. Everywhere affirmations: umbilical-cord roots, angel-wing leaves, symbols of endurance and transcendence in this desolate land, evidence, like my mother's horseshoe, that I, too, was meant to come, that I might still belong to a place I have left behind. I gather my discoveries into a pile.

My mother's voice echoes through the trees. "Where are you? You've got to see this."

I slip the bloodstone in my pocket and follow her voice to the edge of a sandy wash, where I find her and my uncle, hands on their hips, gazing down at their own collections of weathered stones and knotted roots. "Where have you been?" my mother asks. "You've missed everything."

I tell them about the crucifix cactus and the angel-wing leaves. Their faces brighten. They reveal their own discoveries, which will take their place on the tables and shelves of my mother's home: a white pottery shard, a heart-shaped arrowhead, a golden hawk feather, a chunk of cedar as creased as a medicine man's face. Chattering like sage sparrows, they carry their artifacts to the car.

Instead of following, I leave my pile behind and hike toward the sandstone slope above the cave. Cresting the hill, I find my path blocked by a barbed wire fence.

"Oh, no," my mother says, joining me. "This wasn't here last time."

I grab the wire, strung tight as guitar strings.

My uncle stands beside us, arms folded, then walks the length of the chest-high barrier, testing the tension, jiggling the wooden posts, searching for weak spots. Watching him, I notice that the breeze has stilled and the sparrows have stopped darting between branches. We're engulfed by silence, as if the entire llano is holding its breath. I feel exposed suddenly, as if we're doing something wrong, as if we're trespassing, and someone is watching our every move.

"I don't think we should cross."

My uncle steps on the bottom strand. "Why not? We aren't doing anything wrong."

"But someone put this fence here for a reason."

My mother rubs her hands. "Maybe he's right. I don't think I can fit under there."

My uncle pulls up the middle strand while keeping his foot on the bottom, creating a narrow space for us to crouch through. "It's okay. I'll hold it for you. Go ahead."

My mother looks at me, hands me her hat, and lowers herself under.

I survey the hills, once, twice, then follow.

My uncle joins us a second later. Wipes his hands on his jeans.

"That wasn't so bad. Let's have a look inside."

We shuffle onward through the gravel and prickly pear. My mother tugs my shirt.

"Look at this. Bits of china."

She bends to one knee and pinches a shard of porcelain from the sand.

"See the cobalt paint? Probably imported from Spain. And look. Another one. This must have been the original village site."

My uncle joins her. They rake the ground as if searching for loose change.

"You're right. There are pieces everywhere."

I touch the bloodstone in my pocket, acutely aware of our isolation. Once more, I feel the weight of eyes, but the pull of the cave is stronger, and I walk ahead. A dozen yards from the entrance, I see shapes inside: the remnants of whitewashed walls, wooden shelves, a pale blue fresco of Our Lady of Guadalupe—just as my mother described. Again I see Carlos, lips chapped, feet blistered, gazing up from his bedroll at the blessed image, drifting to sleep at last.

I step into the hollow. Behind me, a voice echoes from the village.

"What are you looking for?"

We approach on foot, the road impassable by car, arguing about crossing the fence. "I have a right to be here," my mother bristles. "My family has ties to this land." My uncle nods. "We aren't doing anything wrong. We should go back and get your things." As much as I want to agree with them, I'm still uneasy about the notion of trespassing, of altering the place we're trying to save. I glance across the arroyo at the hillside where I heard the voice echo and stumble over a rock.

"Careful." My mother grabs my shoulder. "The road is dangerous."

She's right. Our path is clogged with granite chunks the size of anvils. What remains of the bridge—busted railroad ties, twisted guard rails, and scraps of corrugated tin—has been washed onto the sandy banks with knots of broken branches, matted grass and uprooted chamisal.

Seeing it and the tight-strung barbed wire I wonder if the barriers are intentional.

"Maybe they don't want visitors," I say.

My mother frowns. "Maybe."

We pick our way through the arroyo and up a hill toward a crumbling stone house. Skirting the edge of the wall, I stumble over the severed head of a cow—eye sockets hollow, black hide peeling from its sun-bleached skull, white teeth clenched in a grin. My mother covers her mouth.

The three men size us up across a weedy field. One wears a red T-shirt, another a blue work shirt, the third a Lakers jersey, their faces shadowed beneath the brims of baseball caps.

The blue shirt says something to the red shirt. They laugh.

After a long silence, my mother cups her hands to her mouth, and in a mix of English and Spanish, shouts the entire story of Carlos' journey across the desert, rattling off family names and birthplaces, introducing my uncle as a priest, and describing me as her wayward son from Denver.

"I brought him here when he was little, but he doesn't remember a thing," she says, throwing her hands in the air. "I'm 72 years old now and I want him to see this land before I die. My father always said he spent one of the most beautiful winters of his life in Marquez. The people here were very kind. They treated him like their own. He never forgot."

The man in red tips back his cap. The others turn to him.

"How did you find us?" he yells.

My uncle shrugs. "My father showed us the way."

The man in red relaxes his shoulders, extends his hand. His grip is strong. Fingers callused. He's short, stocky, probably in his mid-thirties, but with his sunburned skin and crow's feet, appears ten years older. When he smiles, white teeth flash beneath a black mustache.

"Wondered what brought you up here," he says. "I told my cousin, 'This is the first time I've seen anyone up here in a car.' Didn't think you could make it without a truck."

My uncle laughs. "Almost didn't."

The man is a descendent of Enselmo Marquez, whose family once owned every rock and juniper from Mesita del La Madera to the Santa Rosa peaks. Over the years, as ranching became harder, settlers moved east toward the Rio Grande until the century-old village stood empty. He and his cousins live in Albuquerque, but stop by to keep an eye on things. They used to come once a month, then every three months, then sometimes less often. He used to bring his two daughters so they'd remember their roots, but they became too frightened during the sudden storms.

He leans on his shovel. "When the rain comes down, it really comes down. That arroyo you just crossed can go from bone dry to flash flood in seconds. It's like a stampede. You can barely hear yourself talk. And when the lightning hits one of those tin roofs, it sounds like a bomb."

About a year ago, he tells us, the bridge washed out. The state was supposed to fix it, but never did. In fact, just before we arrived, a few workers drove up in a dump truck loaded with lumber and steel, but when they saw the storm clouds, they turned tail and left.

"We worried about that, too," my uncle says. "Getting caught."

The man frowns at the thunderhead to the west. "Might look that way, but it hasn't rained here all summer. Clouds gather around Mount Taylor, then pass us by. And we need rain, too. We've never had such a dry summer. It's weird. But it just won't rain here."

He slips a hand under his cap. Scratches his head. "What was your father's name again?"

My mother repeats the story. The man folds his arms. He's never heard of Carlos Candelaria, but his grandfather did trade with farmers from Corrales. Maybe that was our family. My mother, eager for details, relays what Carlos said about the cave—that it had been an open-air shelter with a potbelly stove, shelves built into the rock, tables, chairs, kerosene lamps and murals of St. Anthony and the Virgin Mary, who gave protection to settlers crossing hostile Navajo and Apache territory.

The man smiles. His companions smile. "True. The cave was a sanctuary."

My mother places a hand on her chest. "I knew it. Your village is blessed."

The man wipes his forehead. "Not anymore. We've lost so much. And we lose more every day. Whenever we visit, something else is gone. Soon, there won't be anything left."

Sweeping a hand over the horizon, he explains how the family land has been steadily carved away by government officials seeking mineral rights, corporate ranchers seeking pasture, hunters seeking hunting grounds. He and his family can't even walk a path they walked for generations.

He points toward the Stetson-shaped hill 200 yards to the north. When he was a boy, his grandfather carried him on his shoulders to a hidden wellspring at the top. Las Palmas, they called it, a pond of clear water surrounded by palms. His family always considered it a sign that settlers had chosen the right spot to live. Each Easter, families climbed the summit to give thanks.

"If I go there now," he says, squaring his shoulders, "I could be prosecuted for trespassing."

His companions grip their shovels. One spits.

But it's not just the government, according to the man in red. Thieves steal, vandals vandalize, black market dealers scavenge the homes for religious art—taking even the church bell.

"A few years ago, they hitched up one of my grandfather's wagons and hauled it away. Me and my cousin found it outside a new restaurant in Albuquerque. Right there with the landscaping. We told them it was ours, but they didn't care. 'Where's your proof,' they said. They don't offer payment. Don't say thanks. They just take it. People come in here and act like this place is theirs."

I feel the bloodstone in my pocket, glance at my mother and uncle, who ignore me.

"They haven't taken everything," I say. "Not yet."

The three of them look at me for the first time.

"True," the red shirt says. "They haven't taken everything."

He gestures to a rectangular building of ochre stones. "That was a post office. My great-grandfather built it a hundred years ago. The floors and windows are gone, but the roof's still there."

He points over my shoulder toward another stone building to the south.

"That was the schoolhouse. Still has walls, windows, roof, everything. They built these homes to last. And with the wind we get out here? The rain? It's a miracle they're standing. Go ahead and look."

We walk over and peek in the school window. The floorboards have buckled, but the tongue-and-groove ceiling is still intact. The walls hold plaster. There's even a blackboard.

Carlos appears: rail thin, tough as cedar, standing before the class with his shy smile, demonstrating the cursive letters the nuns had taught him, adding flourish to his signature "C."

Opposite the blackboard on the south wall, another mark takes shape, a mark snapping me from my daydream—a spray-painted "A," red, with a circle around it. Beside it, a black pentagram.

My uncle folds his arms. "That explains why they haven't had rain. The village is cursed."

The man in blue removes his sunglasses. He's a deacon in Albuquerque. He should have seen the markings, he tells us. He should have known. What should he do?

"Holy water," my uncle says. "Sprinkle the wall."

The man kicks a stone with his boot. "Can you do it, father? Give us a blessing?"

My uncle nods, asks us to join hands, closes his eyes. He prays for the village, for its people, for the rain that won't come, for the difficult tasks before each of us. As he speaks, I wonder, beyond the vandalism, what he means by cursed. The price of forgetting? The affliction of memory?

My mother looks at me.

"Amen."

The man in red checks his watch and glances back at the trench he and his cousins had begun to dig. We shake hands and say goodbye. The three men drag their shovels up the road.

A few miles from the village on the long drive home, my uncle rubs his eyes, parks on the shoulder, and asks my mother for a snack. She doles out cherries, tortillas, chunks of cheddar cheese.

We watch the sky. Thunderheads skirt the village.

"So sad," my mother says. "The New Mexico I knew is gone. All gone."

I spit a pit in my palm. "What about those men?"

"Pobrecitos. I wish I could help them."

"You did. The blessing."

My uncle nods, turns to me. "We should go back for your rocks."

"After what they said? About tourists?"

My mother flips off her sun hat. "We are not tourists. We know the history. The culture. My family has ties here. I'm saving these artifacts, rescuing them, so my grandchildren will know."

"Doesn't seem right."

"But they're beautiful. Let's get them. For your children in Denver. "

"No." My uncle steps out to stretch his legs. "If he doesn't want them, let them be."

My mother turns toward the hill where the man and his grandfather found the wellspring of palms. I follow her eyes. I don't see Carlos, or even a hidden pool, but a shimmer of recognition. And then I see: I am connected to this land by memory, story, her. Perhaps that's the blessing those men truly wanted, the embrace Carlos received. In my mother's pockets, markers of faith.

The car door swings open. My uncle slides behind the wheel. Opens his hand.

"Guess what I found?"

My mother gasps. "A horseshoe. Just like the one we found earlier."

"I didn't even have to look for it," he says. "I opened the car door and there it was. Right in front of me. Sticking up through the dirt in the middle of the road."

I lean forward for a better look. "Quite a coincidence."

He fires the ignition. "There are no coincidences."

Wind blasts the car onto the shoulder of Interstate 40. The sky flashes white.

"Hold on," my uncle says. "We can outrun it."

The speedometer hits 80, 85, 90 . . .

My mother mumbles, tightens her seatbelt.

I slip the bloodstone from my pocket and roll it in my palm. Sand flakes off onto my skin, rusty yellow, fine as pollen. With two fingers, I rub it in.

After a while my uncle glances in the rearview and laughs. "Look at that. Just in time."

Behind us on the horizon, Marquez, blue with rain.

C.L. Prater

The Bones That Were Our People

We saw the signs, small bits of thin black cloth amongst shards of gnawed gold-brown wood, lying on top of the sandy clay soil just as the prairie dog had unearthed them. Their burrow entrances, scattered thinly amongst the cemetery's headstones and wooden crosses, were not round and symmetrical like the mounds beyond the sagging fence, out in open prairie. The fence appeared to be the dividing line between what could be thought of as the active and passive uses of land. There was an irony in following through with that thought for it would be hard to prove which side really was being used in an active sense, the prairie or the cemetery. A nearby prairie dog poked his nose out of his shaded entrance just long enough to catch sight of the large intruders. Producing a squeak of disgust, he quickly disappeared.

This above-ground evidence of the prairie dog's natural or to some unnatural desecration will linger. In an area where vandalism is seen frequently in spray-painted graffiti and plywood-covered broken windows, the cemeteries on the Rosebud Sioux Indian Reservation in south-central South Dakota appear to be less affected. The handwritten note, under a heavy rock, ink washed by rain, is still there. The sun-faded silk flowers, rosary beads and teddy bear with its ribbon shredded by the wind, lie undisturbed on a loved one's grave.

Burial sites are holy places, sacred places in this land, and they have been since the time of the scaffold when the Lakota people placed their dead not in the earth, but on wooden biers high above the ground to aid them in their ascent to the spirit world. It is commonly known that the threat of disease and incoming religious convention eliminated this practice. The final act upon the dead, much changed in direction, has not diminished the sacredness of the place or the holiness of the ground.

The sacredness is instinctive, a natural awareness of the existence of a spirit world. For some, this awareness may come from the stories, passed down from older to younger, of the spirits revealed in ways that can make the telling raise faint hairs on arms and legs in the middle of the day. The ghost stories alone may serve as a deterrent from cemetery mischief yet they may embolden the few wanting to rebel and challenge the local belief system so as to distance themselves from what they believe is a quaint cultural identity.

We walk as carefully over a grave of a hundred years, the headstone of which is unreadable, the slightly depressed earth covered over with prairie, as we do the one which has no marker yet. The mounded earth is still high, the red carnations fragrant, and the leather leaf fern is uncurled. We are careful out of reverence, not fear, knowing that these once-living bodies deserve respect. For some, this respect after death is more than they received in life.

I feel an interaction here though we are separated by time, physical space and earth. As the prairie dog slips into the opening of his burrow I am reminded that there is more than what can be seen above ground, more than just rows of simple stone monuments and weathering wood crosses. Earth envelops wood that houses cloth that drapes the bones that were our people, and still are. These people bore children, spoke sermons, and served drinks in bars. They raised our beef, corrected papers, went to war, and rode bikes with us.

We linger over the graves of young friends and we speak aloud a few thoughts knowing that our memories have been blurred by time. These were the tragedies that thrust mortality at us like a gravel stone hitting a windshield. A friend and I rode bikes with Laura on the summer evening of her death. We stopped at the drive-in restaurant in Mission at the junction of Highways 18 and 83 to talk and get something to drink before heading home. She left heading east and we headed west. I was leaning my bike against a tree in the dusk of our front yard when I heard the sirens. I sat outside until it was fully dark, anticipating something but not wholly expecting it. The call came. Laura had been struck by a car on her way home.

I barely remember Greg. He was a friend of my older brother whose tiny shingle-sided house was across the dirt street from ours. Greg's older half-brother was back to live, at least for a time, with him and his mother. My memories as a six-year-old are of watching the red and blue flashing lights out the window and hearing the lazy screen door that usually closed in its own time being forcefully shut with a snap. The purposeful thud of the heavy wood door and the turn of the bolt were next. I no longer remember the words that were used to tell me the awful news, but whatever they were, they couldn't have had any more impact than the unusual act of my strong wide-shouldered father shutting and locking doors in the dusk of a warm summer evening. Greg and his mother had been murdered with a knife from their kitchen and the brother was gone.

We show respect by how we step and what we say. It doesn't feel right to let our voices intrude too loudly upon this natural stillness. We can't alter the sounds that aren't ours, the rumbling tractor and its plume of diesel exhaust on the nearby road or the occasional scolding of the prairie dogs. We feel we need to walk within hearing distance, to speak to each other in low tones instead of shouting across the stillness. Even the wind, which is a constant here, today causes only a gentle bend in the firmly anchored silk flowers and a slight ripple in the un-mowed native grasses. There are few tree branches for the wind to wail through except for a patchy cedar and plum brush windbreak and an occasional pine that looks misplaced in this bare and ever-so-slight rise, miles from the canyons cut by the ancient flow of the Little White.

A large, heavy locust rests on a flat stone. It is a blush-pink color that I have never seen. I point it out to my siblings and raise my foot to step on it, but my younger brother shakes his head and says gently, "Leave it be." Despite its color and the fact that it is resting on someone's stone like it is safe at home plate, to me it is still an insect that eats gardens. But I understand his unspoken reverence for life in this place of death and let it alone.

A prairie dog barks shrilly in the distance and appears to have come out to roll in the dust. It is said that we began as dust and to that form we will return. I am content with returning to dust. It seems quite natural to return to the basic elements that constitute life. Not long ago we buried our mother. Her shiny casket, the color of canned chokecherry juice, draped with a folded star quilt in plum and lilac colors was elegant and fitting for a woman growing up between the Keya Paha and the Niobrara rivers and raising her children on the Rosebud. When her casket was finally closed it looked like a fortress. A fortress for the newly lifeless, providing the finest in protection when supplemented with its sturdy vault. A prairie dog could never gain entrance. Mom would like that. I don't believe her casket will ever be dust.

It's not meant to. Uncle Lee, my dad's brother, took a totally opposite view. He would have been no more bothered by a prairie dog in his casket than he was with the raccoons and the occasional skunk who took up residence under his four-room house southeast of the town of Rosebud.

Our home town newspaper carried an article a few years ago about the destruction the rodent prairie dogs, carriers of disease and yet beloved pets, caused. A grainy black and white photo in the paper, displayed as best it could the cloth and shards of wood the rodents unearthed. Donations were sought to eradicate the pests and fill the sunken depressions left from their burrows. Before the first snow of the season came that year, the prairie dogs were thought to have been defeated. Surveying the cemetery now, the prairie dogs are back in force, chattering like they've read my thoughts. They won. They have more holes than ever.

Gravel dust loosed by a fast-moving pickup wafts over us and I can't help but breathe in the chalky air. My unvoiced thoughts return to the spiritual. In a family of four children raised in one household our thoughts on after-life issues are different, though mostly in subtle ways that we haven't really discussed all that much. We all have expressed belief in the existence of a world beyond what we see, feel and know. I believe this is true of many, raised like we were, in such a spiritual place as the Rosebud. I personally believe that these lifeless bodies, separated from me only by a few feet of sandy earth, have spirits that have flown to the creator and what is left from these bones and flesh will rise one day in perfection. I also know that my own body, through death, will join in some form with the earth and that the physical time I now try to grasp and hold on to will be no more.

Through an opening in a small mound of earth between flowers and the stone of a woman who died long before I was born lies the tunnel that leads to a prairie dog's den. Maybe this den, a womb in the earth, deep beneath my feet, is a cozy home sided with soft decaying wood. Maybe the prairie dog's babies have a nest in its corner of velvety aged cloth. To me the thought is not detestable. Instead, I am strangely comforted. The prairie dog has in its own way linked two worlds. It is a link, but even more so an interaction, if you will, between the living and the dead.

Mark Rozema

Wherever the Road Goes

Our most necessary preoccupations, obviously, ought to be taking care of one another, of every other person, and of the sweet world and discovering the joy of giving part of one's life away. How to proceed is the question.

—William Kittredge, *from* The Nature of Generosity

My father asks, for the fifth time, if we are on Highway 160. Yes, I tell him. "Why does the road keep changing direction?" he asks. This too is a question he's asked a few times already. Taking my eye off the road just long enough to meet his gaze for a consoling moment, I reply "We're in the mountains, Dad. It's hard to go in a straight line."

My father's eyes are a startling sky-blue, the blue of high desert sky on an October day. I'm tempted to describe them as piercing, which is both a cliché and not quite right. They do not pierce, which is an aggressive verb, and my father is not an aggressive man. But they do hold one's attention. Until recently, I would say that those eyes gave the accurate impression of an agile mind at work—neurons making connections, integrating information, tracing implications, putting together the pieces of the world. They are the eyes of someone who wants, always, to understand. I have seen laughter in his eyes, curiosity, always intelligence and decency—and never have I seen malice, hatred, or duplicity. Sometimes I still see in those eyes an agile mind at work, but too often now his gaze is watery and lost. I see confusion and panic. I sense misfiring neurons, holes into which my words sink and vanish. It is, increasingly, the gaze of a man entering a fog.

We are crossing the Rockies, and he has been trying to read a road map of Colorado. He doesn't know which way to hold the map, much less make sense of it. The red lines, the blue lines, the numbers and symbols and circles... they don't add up to anything that he can discern. This is the man who taught me how to read a map, and passed along to me his love of maps. I wonder if he can put it down, give up on the need to have an abstract representation of the landscape, simply look out the window and notice a mountain, a cloud, a red-tailed hawk, a Lombardy poplar bending in the wind. It's not easy for him to do that. He wants, somehow, for the view out the window and the markings on the paper in his lap to converge, to come sharply into focus in a way that is part mathematical equation and part revelation. He wants the map to locate him.

In his hands, the road map is folded into a small square, revealing only the part of the state that we are in. He fiddles with the map, feeling a need to see the whole state, as if that will make all things suddenly clear. "This is no good," he says, "you have to see the whole thing." He can't quite figure out how the map unfolds, and he tears it. "Why do they make them this way?" he says in frustration. Finally he succeeds in unfolding all of Colorado, but the clarity he sought is still elusive. It seems like a trick, this notion that a piece of paper with lines on it might answer the questions "Where am I? How did I get here? Where do I go next?" Staring at the map with those blue eyes, he says, with great tiredness, "Miles and miles of words . . ."

We pass through Mancos, Durango, Bayfield. Every now and then, he has a memory that is uncannily precise. "This is the Piedra River. We camped here in the old white Chevy. Slept in the truck bed." It is as if a brisk wind had cut through the fog in his mind to reveal a blue pocket of sky, a sharp-edged memory and all the sudden joy that can accompany it. It seems that the names of places bring to him the kind of solace that the map failed to deliver. The amber light of sunset bathes the aspens as we cross Wolf Creek Pass. Names, and the stories that go with them, are like bright stones at the bottom of a creek. As we pass through the San Juan Mountains, I mention place after place, a litany of lakes in which we fished, forest campgrounds where we pitched our funky old tent-trailer, a little town where the alternator gave out on one of our family trips. I don't know how much he remembers, but I want him to feel that the world is sweet and he is part of it.

We are crossing to the east side of the mountains to seek a new home for my parents. My father's dementia has become too hard for my mother to handle on her own. And so, after over fifty years in the land of red rocks and twisted junipers, they are moving in order to live near their eldest daughter, in Fort Collins. It's difficult for me to imagine Arizona without them.

My father has driven Route 160 more times than he could count. Earlier in the day we crossed the Navajo Reservation, where the road elicited from my father no confusion at all. To him—to all of his family—the road from Flagstaff to Cortez is as familiar as a face one sees every day. While it strikes many as a barren emptiness better seen in the rearview mirror, to me it is the landscape of childhood memory, and is therefore beautiful. In particular, the stretch of 160 through Tsegi Canyon always gives me a deep contentment, as if I had slipped into the center of the world. It's a feeling I used to share with my father when we stopped in Tsegi for lunch on hot, dusty summer days, watching slate-blue thunderheads form over Black Mesa, teasing the landscape with the promise of rain.

As a teenager, I used to ride with him in a semi, delivering cases of Pepsi Cola to trading posts and greasy spoons from Gray Mountain to Cameron to Red Lake to Kayenta to Dinnehotso to Baby Rocks to Teec Nos Pos. I loved the days when I could escape the dismal, noisy Pepsi warehouse in Flagstaff, the setting of my first real job, and help him on the Reservation circuit. We stopped at all the trading posts. I loved the easy way in which my father would converse with anyone and everyone, from gruff and hard-headed traders to the skinny Navajo kid on the steps next to a scroungy dog. He moved easily in his skin. I often wondered who, seeing him wheel heavy stacks of soda around and then driving off in his big growling rig, would guess that he was a professor of mathematics. The Pepsi truck was just a summer job.

He does not, anymore, move easily in his skin. Neither does he converse with ease, even with his wife and children. This morning, as we headed north out of Flagstaff, he stared for a long time at the receding profile of the San Francisco Peaks. On the stretch through Tsegi, he was alert and calm; I hoped he felt the peace he and I used to share in that place. It's hard to know. I wondered if he realized that he would never take this road again. It occurred to me that while I see what he sees, I will never see it quite as he does.

After Tsegi, he dozed. As we neared the junction of 160 and 64, he looked out the window at the scattered hogans and cinderblock houses. Then he turned toward me and emphatically blurted out "Teec Nos Pos." It was clear that I was expected to know why this mattered. "Yes," I replied. "Teec Nos Pos." I searched my mind for the significance of this place, until I remembered it. "Tillie Redhouse lived here," I said. He let that fact sink in, as his gaze took in the Carizzo Mountains to the south. "Tillie Redhouse plays the piano," he said, finally, with conviction. He wanted me to know that he still recognized the particulars, the people and places that add up to a life. He wanted to let me know that he was still a participant in the world.

In the years of my growing up, the particulars of my father's work included teaching high school and college, working as a mathematician for the United States Geological Survey, serving as a perpetual elder or deacon at our church, driving a Pepsi truck all over the Navajo Nation, and raising five kids. He was a teacher, mentor, elder, father, husband, and coach. The particulars of his surroundings included the Zuni Indian Reservation, with its dusty pueblo and its sacred mountain, the pine-forested town of Flagstaff, Arizona, also with its sacred mountain, and all the wide sweep of land between.

And he was an intrepid explorer with a curious spirit. When I go back to the child's view of the man with whom I grew up, I see, first of all, his smile. I see it as he drives with one sunburned arm out the window. I don't know if anything pleased my father more than a plain red-dirt track into wide-open country. It became a family joke, my father's oft-repeated phrase: "I wonder where this road goes . . ." My mother's exasperated response was also a source of amusement to us: "It's just a road, Wes, like any other road. Do we have to know where every road goes?" If he was driving, the answer was yes, apparently we did. His inquiry may have been disingenuous; more often than not, he already had a good idea where the road would go. But why not take it anyway, just to be sure? What better way to spend an afternoon? Why not take a watermelon, a fishing pole, the Coleman stove, a can of Spam, and just see where the road goes?

Wesley James Rozema didn't know where the road would take him when, in 1952, he left his home in Michigan, spurred westward by asthma and a curious spirit. Like so many others in the middle of the past century, he followed Route 66, headed for California with his young wife and two daughters. But there was a lot of country between Michigan and California, and that country laid claim on him. My parents passed the Twin Arrows Trading

Post, where a billboard as big as a movie screen proclaimed "See a real live Indian!" In Holbrook, they stayed in a motel of cheesy concrete tipis. Between Gallup and Flagstaff, it seemed he could see forever across the wide sweep of cinder hills, volcanic diatremes, sandstone buttes, dusky blue mountains, and the caliche hills of the Painted Desert. After an unsatisfactory dalliance with California, my folks returned to this land of endless sky and wind and dirt roads, eventually settling in Flagstaff, where my father landed a job at Northern Arizona University as a professor of mathematics.

He might not, while wheeling heavy stacks of pop around a trading post, be easily mistaken for a professor—but then, he was perhaps an unusual professor. I have memories of waiting outside his office for what seemed like hours while he helped students. I recall the day he helped a tearful Navajo girl who protested that she was "too stupid" to do math. I remember how he put her at ease with some chat about places and people. Perhaps when she discovered that he knew who ran the trading post at Chilchinbito, she was surprised and suddenly didn't feel quite as alone at the big university. And before he turned her attention to the equations, he let her know, in a subtle and understated way, that he considered herding a flock of sheep through a labyrinth of canyons and deep sand to be every bit as challenging as mastering differential equations. In short, he treated her as an equal and assumed she was interesting and capable.

My father helped many students who went back to the Reservation to become teachers themselves. In the 1970s Northern Arizona University began a concerted effort to prepare primary and secondary teachers to teach in reservation schools. Few math teachers at that time were Native American, and the retention rate for Native students was low. The university wanted to find someone who could effectively prepare primarily Navajo, Hopi, Apache and Zuni undergrads to become science and math teachers. My father was chosen to direct this program. I know he considers the time spent training these teachers among the most important contributions he has made in his lifetime.

But before he was a professor, he was a high school teacher. In 1955, after determining that the suburbs of Los Angeles were not to his liking, he found his way back to the high desert when a job opened up on the Zuni Reservation in New Mexico. His job would be to teach mathematics to Zuni teenagers. Back then, the pueblo did not have a paved street, a stop sign, a grocery store, or a hospital. People cooked in outdoor clay ovens. Zuni had few white residents. The preparation my father had for this job was a degree in Math with a minor in Choral Music from a Dutch Calvinist Christian college in Michigan. He had probably not ever eaten a chile or seen a rattlesnake. To my knowledge, he had no preparation in cross-cultural communication or cultural anthropology. He was a stranger in a strange land.

They put him straight to work. He was a warm body. He taught math, of course, and directed the choir. He also taught health, physical education, Earth science, physics, and surely some courses I can't recall. He coached basketball, track and cross-country. I've seen pictures of a man with a severe flat-top brush cut and a whistle standing next to a track team of wiry boys with names like Alvin Owelagte and Estevan Quam. I've listened to a scratchy vinyl recording of his choir singing Handel. I try to imagine his life.

Just as my life began in red dirt, my father's life began in black dirt. I remember him speaking of wading through the black muck of his grandfather's celery farm in Michigan. I barely remember his parents and the wider community of which he was a part—Dutch Calvinists, hard-headed Frisians, ice skaters and farmers, with names like Veenstra, Rozema. I imagine my father as a teenager reciting the questions and answers to the Heidelberg Catechism. I've seen pictures of him from college, singing in barbershop quartets, playing the double bass. Can I really comprehend the scope of his journey?

The journeys of the generations dovetail. My earliest memory is of playing in the dirt at the Christian Reformed Mission in Zuni. Maybe I cried, because some lady who smelled of peppermints scooped me up and brushed me off. I remember also the smell of juniper smoke from the ovens and of sitting in my father's lap, wrapped in a blanket, as we watched from the pueblo rooftop as the procession of dancers entered the plaza. I have written a poem about this, which, like many poems, is a small thread of memory braided with a larger thread of imagination, because, of course, I can't really remember what my four-year-old self thought. The dream is made up, but the feeling from which this poem comes—the clear sense of incarnation and the sense that the Shalako embodied a mystery—was not.

Shalako

Back to the beginning: Zuni, New Mexico,
December, 1966. A four-year-old boy swaddled
in a blanket, sitting on an adobe roof, waiting
for the Shalako. Perched on rooftops
around the plaza, everyone in Zuni waits,
solemn and expectant. Then, out of a whirlwind
of red dust, he emerges, long beak snapping.
Is a man behind the mask? the young boy asks.
Yes and no. God puts on a body.
The shuffle of kachina dancers in dust, pulse
of rattles and bells, and the constant chanting
lull the boy into a dream: there is no ground
or sky, but only whiteness and he is in it,
floating, as the towering Shalako bends down
low as if to swallow him up, but instead
reaches out and plants a seed in the boy's head.
When he wakes, the boy stares at his tiny hand
as he flexes and unflexes it into a fist.
God puts on a body! Anything can happen.

Like my father wondering about the road ahead, I'm not sure where these reminiscences are leading. Landscape and story, body and spirit intertwined. God puts on a body. Maybe this is true of us all and not just the Shalako. Old-fashioned Dutch Calvinists are embarrassed by bodies—their hungers, their weaknesses. Bodies lead to sin, bodies age, bodies give out. My father's hands are old, weak now, the skin mottled and papery. They were not always so. A disease is crippling his brain, and this was not always so. Still, the mild man who is my father shines brightly in both body and spirit. Can we see the sacred in the fleeting world?

Here is another story, a truer one than the poem, although the details are fuzzy. My father told me this story many years ago, and I didn't recognize (as young people fail sometimes to recognize) that it was a story that mattered.

My father described to me a conversation he had with a twelve-year-old boy on his track team as they rode together on a long bus trip. They were talking about Zuni religion—always a delicate subject. My father wondered how the Shalako made his wooden beak snap so sharply. Was there a mechanism in the mask? The twelve-foot-tall Shalako is one of the most beloved and important kachina spirits, which inhabit the bodies of men in ceremonial dances. It has a long wooden "beak" or "clapper" that makes startling noises, perhaps to keep young Zuni children from falling asleep.

My father was never one to embellish stories. His telling of the tale was sparse, leaving much to speculation. He remembered that the boy hesitated at such an invasive question, and stared hard at his coach. I imagine the boy to be sizing up this white man. What is he after? Is he making fun of me? In the boy's hesitation, my father found a way to say to the boy that he meant no disrespect; he understood that the dancer in the Shalako mask was filled with the spirit of the Shalako, and that he was, at the same time, a man. In wondering about how the beak worked, he was merely curious, but he didn't question that a Shalako spirit was involved. The boy was silent for a while. It was not unusual for Zuni kids to be silent. But then he opened up. He told my father, almost apologetically, that he didn't know what made the beak snap. Then he added that he knew it sounded crazy to a white man, but what he and all Zunis believed was that the kachinas came out of the salt lake and entered into the bodies of Zuni men.

In 1955, cultural sensitivity toward Native people was not great, and among white people there was not the widespread respect toward Native spirituality that there is today. The "wanna-be" tribe was much smaller in number. I don't think Zunis were accustomed to whites being anything but dismissive of their religion. Anthropologists were patronizing, seeing Zuni faith as something to be studied, while missionaries were hostile, seeing Zuni faith as something to be conquered. My father, an evangelical Christian new to the reservation and with no particular insight into Zuni ways, simply saw before him a boy who had entered into an awkward conversation with a white teacher about things that probably ought not to be talked about. My dad assured the boy that it didn't sound crazy at all. He said that his own religion also taught that spirits can inhabit people. And the conversation went no further. One of the things my father understood was when to stop. I don't suppose there was anything remarkable in the content of my father's words, but something in his manner allowed that boy to be both open and vulnerable.

After almost a decade in Zuni, my father moved his family to Arizona, where he finished his Master's degree, and then became an Assistant Professor at Northern Arizona University. This was in the days when it was still possible to get such a position without a PhD. In his thirty-five year career, I think he held the dubious distinction of being the last remaining professor in the math department without a PhD. Had he come seeking a job ten years later, he would not have been hired. He didn't often publish in mathematical journals; he had no interest in it. He was a college professor who still believed that teaching was the most important task. He was hired when NAU still wore the old-fashioned label of "Teacher's College."

Throughout my father's life, I have seen in him a willingness to step forward and do whatever needs to be done. In our church, he was a perpetual elder and organizer of projects. He did the work, whatever it was: balancing the finances, painting, roofing the sanctuary, cutting wood for the pastor. And he did the work with a generous spirit, with humility, kindness, and humor. He didn't toot his own horn. In fact, he never thought highly of himself. He considered himself ordinary at best. Growing up under his roof, I thought he was ordinary too. It took a while to discover otherwise.

After he retired from teaching, and was well into his seventies, he served on the board of directors for the relief society of his church. In this capacity, he traveled to places like Malawi and Nicaragua, where he worked on projects that involved AIDS and malaria prevention, poverty reduction, microlending, agricultural sustainability, and clean water. In our own country, he went with work teams to areas affected by disasters: flooding in South Texas and California, rebuilding and needs assessment in Louisiana after Hurricane Katrina. In Malawi he caught malaria and nearly died; his stamina was greatly reduced after that. When at age 76 he shared with me a slideshow of his trip to Africa, I was struck by his rambling and inarticulate manner; this was new to him. I began to worry.

Five years ago, he was hiking the red rocks of Oak Creek with a spring in his step; two years ago, he could barely make his legs get him up to the top of the mesa from which he surveyed the wide sweep of high desert in which he has spent most of his life. He spoke to me, then, of the ways in which I have taught him: He has in the past twenty years read many of the books I send him—especially those with an ecological theme. In response, he said, "I never thought about any of that stuff when I was younger." What he didn't realize is that it all came from him. The love of nature, the love of the world, and the love of people, especially people who are on the margins of society—it all came from him.

Now he is moving into a time of life in which nothing makes sense. The road ahead frightens rather than draws him forward. His logical, linear mind is failing him. He feels that he is a burden to his wife and children. The math teacher no longer balances the checkbook. The driver of big rigs has relinquished his keys.

Light is fading as we drop down the east side of Wolf Creek Pass into the town of Del Norte, where forty years ago the alternator gave out and our family spent the day in a park. He remembers that. To me it was a carefree afternoon to roughhouse with my brother under the locust trees. I didn't worry; cars were grown-up stuff. I didn't know till much later that my dad was flummoxed by car trouble. I didn't know that parents could feel anxiety. What I did know was that I was in my father's care, and that was sufficient.

Now I am about the age that my father was on that hot August day in Del Norte. I have children and parents, and responsibility stretches in both directions. I hope that my care is sufficient. We are all in a web of reciprocal relationships, and I know now that the strands connecting us are more tenuous than I once thought. How do we give back to those who have sustained us with love and generosity? The way is not clear, and how to proceed is indeed the question. There is no map that charts the course.

As we leave Del Norte, the last faint glow of sunset slips off of the tops of the Sangre de Cristo Range. Travelling at night will make my father anxious, so in the next town we will get a motel. He will wake up in the middle of the night, wondering where he is and why everything is strange to him. Nights are the hardest time. He will ask me where we are going, and I will say—as I've said before—"Fort Collins. A new home." This answer will be of less consequence than what follows: "I'm with you, Dad. Your whole family is with you." Wherever the road goes.

Roz Spafford

The Indian

Bud's presence in our lives only became a mystery later, once I grew up. When I was a child, he was as permanent as a parent and as familiar. I was curious about a few things—why he insisted on using the outhouse rather than the indoor bathroom and where he went when he went off on foot and where some of his teeth had gone. But I never wondered why he lived with us part of each year once he had sold the ranch to us, rather than with his son and daughter-in-law who ran a motel in town, what his wife in southern Arizona thought of his long absences, and whether my mother found him to be a companion or a trial.

The time I might have asked him these questions closed in the early seventies, when he died. I might have asked my parents before they died, but I did not ask. It used to be that when I thought about the ranch, I returned to childhood and did not question how things were.

Bud must have been between 70 and 80 when he lived with us off and on. He worked like a much younger man, though he walked like one who had been thrown from a horse too many times—butt tucked under, back stiff. A hand-rolled cigarette clung to his lower lip and he chewed his words.

Bud renamed everyone: My father was Bill, though his name was Roy. My mother was Mrs. Bill. His daughter-in-law was Boy and his grandson was Bubby. My sister was Louisita. I was the Indian.

I am not, in any way, an Indian, and he was, though perhaps in ways more complex than we knew then, so I took the renaming as the honor it was. I was too young to know how troublesome it was for a white girl on what was rightfully Indian land to be called an Indian. At age five, at nine, it gave me an alternative standard to live up to: I would be brave. I would resist oppression. I would study the land. I would follow Bud from corral to barn, barn to shed, shed to yard, and learn to pound jerky and vaccinate a calf. Because—for reasons I do not understand—Bud was sometimes at home when my father was out on horseback riding the fences or checking the waters, he anchored the outdoor world where I could be away, safe from my mother. I needed that alternative: My mother was determined that I would be a musician and many of her efforts went toward making sure that I would not grow up to do ranch work or marry a cowboy. The name gave me license to be at home on the land without overtly challenging my mother's ambitions for me; it eased the sting of not being tough and competent like the ranch girls who rode in rodeos, as I would never have been allowed to do. When I was "the Indian," I was not a hostage in the war between my parents, nor could I be assimilated into the town culture I encountered at school.

Bud had also renamed himself—or someone had renamed him, possibly more than once. As a child, I never knew his real first name and I only know it now because a historian who interviewed him published it while acknowledging that he should not have. I am not, for that reason, fully naming him here, as I am not sure he would want me to.

Only once as a child did I have a sense of Bud as a person with secrets. My father was excavating under the bathroom, perhaps dealing with pipes that had broken during the winter, and discovered a skeleton, perfectly intact, laid out respectfully. Asked by the sheriff what he knew about it, Bud simply looked enigmatic.

The skeleton was not the only reminder that people had preceded us on the ranch. On a flat patch of ground by the well, I would find square-headed nails from another era, purple glass. The story at the time was that it took a hundred years for glass to turn purple, but like so much else, it was not true; in the 1850s, a hundred years before we lived there, the Hualapai people had not yet been removed from the land that became the ranch. When we were there, the only sign that they or their predecessors had been there was a ring of rocks around a fire pit at the top of the hill I used to climb, rocks with white pictographs on them. Some days I could find the ring; other days I could not.

To call them Hualapai is to rename them. "Hualapai" is an Anglo misunderstanding of Amat Whala Pa'a, one of the thirteen Pai bands that eventually became the Hualapai Nation, and the one that lived and moved across what became the ranch. They were assumed to be one people by those who coveted the six million acres in northwestern Arizona that were their territory. Later, as Jeffrey Shepherd points out in his 2010 book, *We Are an Indian Nation,* shared suffering and political acumen led them to accept the collective identity of the Hualapai Nation.

Like Bud, all of us on the ranch were divided. My father was an artist as well as a rancher; my mother was an urban working-class East Coast woman living in primitive conditions that must have astonished her. She played opera on the hi-fi once we got power, took correspondence courses in psychology and literature through Arizona State, longed for a life centered on the mind, not the worn, exhausted body. I was the fraying rope in the tug-of-war between the life my mother lived and the one she dreamed of, the life we lived and the one she would have for me. Contained in that little house, apparently built by someone without a plumb line since everything was askew, all four of us had the privilege of moving amongst multiple worlds and, at the same time, struggled with the cost of being at war with ourselves.

My mother's longings were the loudest; I would not have been permitted to describe feeling taut as a rope, the strands splitting. It would have been ungrateful. Whether my father longed for his painting studio when he was rounding up cattle, I don't know. And what price Bud paid for being divided, however he was divided, I will never know.

Bud's gifts to me were profound: He was the only grandparent I knew, as my parents' parents were far away. As a child, I met each one only once or twice, and though they wrote, they were not real to me. Bud was entirely real, his tobacco smell, his muttered speech, his suspenders hardly holding up his pants, his praise of me in the third person: "Oh, that Indian, he built another fine little camp today, out there under the cliffs by the sand wash." Bud referred to me as "he," and I thought of myself as "he," until I had to think otherwise. Unlike my parents, Bud did not require that I *be* some idealized version of him, even though he had, in that odd sense, named me after himself.

Perhaps because Bud was not actually a parent, he gave me a world in which I was not evaluated continuously against an unreachable standard. I do not remember him ever correcting me or criticizing me—only his approval of my wandering the property, feeding an orphaned calf, setting up the little "camps," as he called them, where in my imagination I was a country doctor saving a child or an Indian fighting to save my people or a cowboy warning a village against a flash flood.

While in our play as children and in the real world around us, cowboys and Indians were at odds, Bud was both cowboy and Indian, as were the Apache of the generations before him, renowned as cattlemen. Likewise, once the Hualapai could no longer live the migratory life that had once supported them, some became ranchers—though their right to occupy even reservation land was continually challenged while local ranchers were permitted to run their own cattle across Hualapai territory. The Hualapai were remarkable in many respects; forced in 1874 to relocate from their ancestral lands to an unlivable site in the Sonora desert, those who survived escaped in 1875 and made their way back, a trek now commemorated each year in the La Paz run, when the Hualapai run north from where they were interned. As Shepherd explains it, they continued to resist colonization, including filing—and winning—a suit against the Santa Fe Railroad which was encroaching on their land, and insisting that the residential school their children were required to attend be located on the Hualapai reservation, enabling them to protect their children and preserve their culture, at least to some degree

These wars, internal and external, were not visible to me as a child. My father had enormous admiration for what he understood of Native American cultures and respect for the Hualapai people in our community, and he understood full well that white invaders had taken that way of life and indeed the lives themselves. But lost in the romantic vision of the cowboy and overwhelmed by the exhaustion and anxiety of that world, he did not locate himself as one of them – perhaps because he had bought, not taken, the ranch from a Native American, perhaps because the price—not just monetary—was so high, perhaps because he could not endure the contradiction.

In this sense, he was like many of us in today's landscape: We mourn what has been done to the natural world and are outraged by the ways the poor in our own countries and elsewhere suffer so that we can have what we have. It is difficult to stay continually aware that we have what we have because it was taken from someone else; when, like my father, we struggle at home and at work, it doesn't feel like privilege. And I am sure that my father, bone-tired after 12 hours riding in sun, coming home to a hopeful child and a wife once again mysteriously angry, did not feel like an occupier.

Bud's presence, his advice on what the land and animals needed, his kindness to me, cast an approving light on us and all we did. It might be that he in fact approved of us; my father was honorable in his dealings with people and I expect that he accepted Bud's guidance gratefully. Bud ran a few cattle on the ranch, ate dinner with us, and told stories late into the night. He never treated us as intruders, though we were living in the house that had been his own, working the land he had sold to us. He wrote to us regularly and warmly after we moved to California. Thus my father might have felt as if we had "the Indian's" blessing to be there.

Of course I understand that he could not have blessed us on behalf of all Native Americans, not just because he was not descended from one of the Hualapai peoples who had lived on the land in the previous forever. No one can be a spokesman for a whole group unless he has been asked to be so—but Bud's approval might be how my father, who was acutely sensitive to injustice and grieved by the way Native Americans had been torn from their land, might have still felt entitled to live on it.

Even Bud's heritage is a mystery now. Then we knew he was half Apache, with all the gifts we thought came with it—to track a deer, manage a bad horse, tell a good story. But genealogical records show his father to have been a white military man and rancher who had been what was called then an Indian scout and his mother a German immigrant who died when he was a baby—though one of these facts might not be true. That is, his father was among those men who "scouted" Apaches who resisted the white occupation and refused to stay on the reservation. In the course of this bloody, dangerous, wretched work, Apaches themselves, supervised by people like Bud's father, were hired to locate and capture their own countrymen.

The bones of Apache people killed in one of his father's raids in 1874 were visible from the ranch his father established in Aravaipa Canyon shortly afterward, according to a memoir by Bud's brother. Aravaipa was also the site of the 1871 massacre of over a hundred sleeping Apaches, mostly women and children, by white and Mexican Tucson elites (including the future mayor) and their Tohono O'odham allies. Twenty-nine children were kidnapped in that raid, some sold into slavery in Mexico, some placed with prominent Tucson families and never returned, according to Chip Colwell-Chanthaphonh's 2007 book *Massacre at Camp Grant*. By the time Bud was born in 1880, some Apache families had returned to the Canyon.

So was Bud kidnapped from an Apache family in some later raid? If so, what did "half Apache" mean? Was he the result of an alliance between Bud's father and a neighboring Apache woman, a baby claimed and brought back to the ranch to live? It is a mystery—and neither his brother's memoir nor family records shed any light on it. Bud certainly knew his father's history—a letter he wrote to a researcher in 1958 indicates that by the age of 9, he was well-acquainted with the most famous of the white Apache scouts, and he must have known that his father was involved in the 1885 campaign against Geronimo.

In claiming an Apache identity (half Apache, he always specified), Bud might have been speaking literally or he might have taken on that identity out of respect or something more complicated. What must it have meant to have carried, literally or metaphorically, the identity of the people his father had killed, the people whose bones lay out in the sun near his home?

No one took pictures of me and Bud together. There are pictures of me with my parents and me alone or with a colt; there are pictures of Bud standing with a rope in a corral, hog-tying a calf, staring into the distance. A picture would have shown me trotting behind him; I do not recall riding with him or talking face-to-face—I remember always seeing him from an angle. I learned from Bud to be quiet in the world of land and animals. For me, every piñon pine, prickly-pear cactus, red-rock cliff, every piece of quartz was—and then there are no words, certainly none Bud would have said. "Sentient" is almost the right word, as I felt the trees had mind, were aware. The rocks seemed less aware, but for me they were in some sense holy. I gathered rock after rock, had boxes full.

Is there a language in which this does not sound foolish? This sensibility may follow inevitably from walking through the land for hours as a small child, mostly alone. Sequestered from vigorous ranch work by my father because I was a girl and might get hurt, by my mother because I was destined for a different future and she was worried about my hands, what I was allowed to do was wander, as long as I had a dog with me. I talked to the cedar trees and believed they answered. I set up rock arrangements as if they were shrines. I studied the glistening mica grains in the black volcanic sand.

The only person whose presence on the land resembled mine was Bud, who—likely because he did not have to keep the ranch afloat—spent some time himself wandering or just looking. My father loved the land but was at odds with it, trying to coax a livelihood out of it. His love for it is apparent in his paintings; the horse and cowboy are always in the center, but the landscape they are placed in is most lovingly painted. My mother, too, found the land beautiful but she would not have been losing herself in it, wrung dry as she was by the hardship and what must have been the continuing shock of conditions there. Both my parents suffered at the land's hands, while I did not.

I did not say goodbye to Bud when we left; he must have been at his own place in southern Arizona. Six years of drought had left the ranch a graveyard of cattle; my parents, like so many before them, thought that a better life would be possible in California. They did not tell me we would not be coming back until we were already in California, so as we were leaving I did not know I was saying goodbye to Bud, to that land—saying goodbye to myself.

CONTRIBUTORS

Contributor Notes

A Delaware native, **Nina Bennett** is the author of *Sound Effects* (2013, Broadkill Press Key Poetry Series chapbook #4). Her poetry has appeared in numerous journals and anthologies such as *Kansas City Voices, Big River Poetry Review, Houseboat, Bryant Literary Review, Yale Journal for Humanities in Medicine, Philadelphia Stories,* and *The Broadkill Review.* Nina was a 2012 Best of the Net nominee.

Peter Bridges spent three decades as a Foreign Service officer, ending as American ambassador to Somalia. Kent State University Press has published his *Safirka: An American Envoy; Pen of Fire: John Moncure Daniel;* and *Donn Piatt: Gadfly of the GIlded Age.* His shorter work has appeared in *California Literary Review, Michigan Quarterly Review, Virginia Quarterly Review,* and elsewhere.

Joe Carvalko, writes across a wide variety of genres including fiction, non-fiction and poetry. Some of his most recently published works are *We Were Beautiful Once, Chapters from the Cold War* (novel, Sunbury Press, 2013); *The Techno-human Shell—A Jump in the Evolutionary Gap* (nonfiction, Sunbury Press, 2012); and *The Science and Technology Guidebook for Lawyers* (ABA Publishing, May, 2014). "The Road Home" was a finalist, (Esurance Poetry prize, 2012). He holds a BSEE, MFA (writing), and a JD.

Will Cordeiro is completing his Ph.D. in English at Cornell University. His recent work appears or is forthcoming in *burnt district, Cortland Review, Crab Orchard Review, Drunken Boat, Phoebe,* and elsewhere. He lives in Tucson, Arizona.

David Lavar Coy has published poems in previous anthologies of *Manifest West,* one nominated for a Pushcart Prize. His poetry books include *Rural News, Lean Creatures,* and *Down Time to Tombstone* (with David Tammer). He is a former professor at Arizona Western College and has an MFA from the University of Arkansas, in Fayetteville, 1983.

Harrison Candelaria Fletcher is the author of *Descanso for My Father: Fragments of a Life,* winner of a 2013 Colorado Book Award and Independent Book

Publisher Award Bronze Medal. His work has appeared in *New Letters, Fourth Genre, The Touchstone Anthology of Contemporary Creative Nonfiction,* and many other journals. He teaches in Virginia Commonwealth University's MFA Program.

John Haggerty's work has appeared widely in magazines such as *Confrontation, Nimrod, Salon,* and *The Santa Monica Review,* and is the recipient of the 2013 Pinch Literary Prize. He is currently putting the finishing touches on his novel *Calamity Springs,* which was a finalist for the 2013 James Jones First Novel Fellowship.

Chad Hanson serves as chairman of the Department of Sociology & Social Work at Casper College. His creative nonfiction titles include *Swimming with Trout* and *Trout Streams of the Heart.* His first full-length collection of poems, *Patches of Light,* won the 2013 David Martinson-Meadowhawk Prize. The book is available from Red Dragonfly Press.

Duane L. Herrmann, 1989 recipient of Robert Hayden Poetry Fellowship, lives on the rolling Kansas prairie. He is the author of a major collection of poetry: *Prairies of Possibilities.* His poetry is included in *American Poets of the 1990s,* CYCLAMENSANDSWORDS.COM, *Flint Hills Review,* KANSASPOETS. COM, LITERARYYARD.COM, *Little Balkans Review, Midwest Quarterly, Orison, Planet Kansas, Kansas Poets Trail, Whirlwind Review, Map of Kansas Literature* (website), and elsewhere.

M.E. Hope has been a Fishtrap Fellow, a Playa Resident, and was awarded an Individual Artist Fellowship from the Oregon Arts Commission in 2013. Her chapbook, *The past is clean,* was published by Uttered Chaos in 2010. In 2013 she moved back to Europe, and is busy examining the Belgium sky and missing hummingbirds.

William Hudson was born in Arkansas, grew up both there and in Illinois, lives now in Spokane, where he worked many years for a community action agency. He has appeared in *The Caribbean Writer, HEArt Journal, Review Americana, DMQ Review, The View From Here, New Madrid Review, The Honey Land Review, Pif Magazine, The Other Journal,* and elsewhere.

Marc Janssen cut his teeth in the vibrant Ventura poetry scene where he learned that his poem really isn't done until it is read aloud. His work is scattered around the Internet, print journals, and anthologies. Poetry, work, education, soccer, kids, wife, love, church, drums, angst, kayaking: pretty boring really.

Don Kunz taught literature, creative writing, and film studies at the University of Rhode Island for 36 years, retiring as Professor Emeritus. His essays, short stories, and poems have appeared in over 70 journals. He lives in Bend Oregon where he volunteers, writes, studies Spanish, and plays Native American Flute.

Ellaraine Lockie's recent poetry has been awarded the 2013 Women's National Book Association's Poetry Prize, Best Individual Collection from *Purple Patch* magazine in England for "Stroking David's Leg," winner of the San Gabriel Poetry Festival Chapbook Contest for *Red for the Funeral* and *The Aurorean*'s Chapbook Pick for *Wild as in Familiar*. She teaches poetry workshops and serves as Poetry Editor for the lifestyles magazine, *Lilipoh*

Rebecca Pelky lives in Marquette, Michigan, on the south shore of Lake Superior, where she is an instructor and MFA candidate in poetry at Northern Michigan University. Her work has appeared or is forthcoming in *Prick of the Spindle, Stone Highway Review*, and *Yellow Medicine Review*, among others.

C.L. Prater is a teacher of young students with special needs. Born on the Yakama Reservation in Washington State, she grew up on the Rosebud Reservation of South Dakota and now lives in northeast Nebraska with her husband, children and grandchildren. She writes, gardens, and keeps the grass mowed around a half mile of young chokecherry bushes.

Mark Rozema's nonfiction has recently appeared in *Flyway, Sport Literate, Weber: The Contemporary West, Under the Sun, Isthmus, The Soundings Review*, and elsewhere. His first book, *Road Trip*, is forthcoming from Boreal Books, an imprint of Red Hen Press. He lives in Shoreline, Washington with his wife, daughter, and dogs. He enjoys working in the garden, climbing mountains, and competing in track & field.

Scot Siegel lives in Oregon where he works as a city planner. His most recent book of poems is *Thousands Flee California Wildflowers* (County Clare, Ireland: Salmon Poetry, 2012).

Jared Smith is the author of eleven volumes of poetry. He is a Board Member of *The New York Quarterly*, and Poetry Editor of *Turtle Island Quarterly*. He's served on the Editorial Boards of *Home Planet News, The Pedestal*, and *Trail & Timberline*. Jared lives near Boulder, and maintains a cabin deep in the woods of Roosevelt National Forest.

Roz Spafford was raised on a cattle ranch in northwestern Arizona. "The Indian" is part of her memoir-in-progress about that life. For many years, she taught writing at the University of California, Santa Cruz; she now works as a writing instructor at the University of Toronto. Her book of poems, *Requiem*, was awarded the 2008 Gell Poetry Prize from Writers & Books. Her short story, "Drought," received the 2010 David Nathan Meyerson award from *Southwest Review*.

Scott T. Starbuck, a 2013 Artsmith Fellow on Orcas Island, feels destruction of Earth's ecosystems is related to spiritual illness and widespread urban destruction of human consciousness. A former charter captain and commercial fisherman turned creative writing professor, his newest book, *The Other History*, published by FutureCycle, is at AMAZON.COM. He blogs about environmental issues, fishing, and poetry at RIVERSEEK.BLOGSPOT.COM.

Alex L. Swartzentruber is a writer from Indiana. He currently resides in Brooklyn, New York. He writes every day and does pushups every day.

Pepper Trail's poetry has appeared in *Comstock Review, Atlanta Review, Spillway, Kyoto Journal, Borderlands, Windfall,* and other publications, and his environmental essays are published regularly in *High Country News*. Trail lives in Ashland, Oregon, where he works for the U.S. Fish and Wildlife Service. *Hydrology, Northern Great Basin* was written during a writer's residency at Playa, on the shores of Summer Lake, Oregon.

Miles Waggener is the author of two poetry collections: *Phoenix Suites* (The Word Works, 2003), winner of the Washington Prize; and *Sky Harbor* (Pinyon

Publishing, 2011); as well as two chapbooks *Portents Aside* (Two Dogs Press, 2008) and *Afterlives* (Finishing Line Press, 2013). He lives in Omaha.

Tim Weed's collected stories have been shortlisted for the New Rivers Press Many Voices Project, the Autumn House Fiction Prize, and the Lewis-Clark Press Discovery Award. He is a lecturer in the MFA Writing program at Western Connecticut State University and a featured expert for National Geographic Expeditions in Cuba, Spain, and Patagonia.

Sarah Brown Weitzman, a Pushcart nominee, has had over three hundred poems published in numerous journals such as *America, The North American Review, Art Times, Rattle, The Mid-American Review, The Windless Orchard, Slant, Poet Lore, Potomac Review,* and others. Weitzman received a Fellowship from the National Endowment for the Arts and the 2013 Harry Hoyt Lacey Poetry Prize. Her latest book, a children's novel, *Herman and the Ice Witch,* was published by Main Street Rag in 2011.

Barbara Yost was an award-winning newspaper feature writer for many years and now works as a freelance newspaper, magazine and fiction writer in Phoenix. She has degrees in English and Journalism from the University of Iowa, a master's degree in English from Arizona State University, and an MFA in creative writing from Arizona State. Her short stories and poems have been published in *Roar,* the Los Gatos anthology, *Prism Review,* the *Valparaiso Fiction Review,* and Best Short Stories from the *Saturday Evening Post* Great American Fiction Contest 2014.

About the Editors and Designer

Larry K. Meredith, Director of the Publishing Certificate Program at Western State Colorado University, previously served as Western's Assistant to the President and Director of Public Relations. He has been a newspaper man, a salesman, an advertising and sales promotion writer for a Fortune 500 company, director of a library district and has owned his own marketing and video production firm. He is the author of the historical novel *This Cursed Valley* (2012) and has another novel and a biography with a literary agent. His publishing company, Raspberry Creek Books, Ltd., was formed to publish books that "celebrate the American West."

Laura Anderson is a writer and editor for the *Gunnison Country Times*, in which she has published countless articles. She is the editor of the *Gunnison Country Magazine*. She holds a Bachelor of Arts in English as well as a Certificate in Publishing from Western State Colorado University. Laura spends her weekends writing and exploring the beautiful Colorado valley she calls home.

Jennifer L. Gauthier has a B.A. in Letters, which covered the topics of language, writing, literature, philosophy, and history from the University of Oklahoma and a publishing certificate from Western State Colorado University. She is completing an internship with the Montrose (Colorado) *Daily Press*. Her love of writing began at age 9, and she recently produced her first novel, *Among the Threads of Time* (self-published in 2014). Currently she is completing and editing her second novel.

A.J. Sterkel has a B.A. in English from the University of Colorado Denver and a publishing certificate from Western State Colorado University. Before working as an associate editor for *Manifest West*, she worked as an editorial assistant for *Copper Nickel Literary Journal*. She is a MFA student in the Writing for Children and Young Adults program at Spalding University. She lives in Colorado and is writing a young adult novel.

Russell Davis is a bestselling author with numerous novels and short stories, under a wide variety of pseudonyms, to his credit. He teaches fiction in the MFA program at Western State Colorado University. His most recent collection is *The End of All Seasons*, and you can learn more by visiting his website at MORNINGSTORMBOOKS.COM.

David J. Rothman serves as Director of the MFA in Creative Writing at Western. He is Poet-in-Residence for Colorado Public Radio. His next book will be *Go Big*, a collection of poems due from Red Hen Press in 2015.

With a doctorate in English from Texas Tech University, **Mark Todd** has served on the faculty at Western State Colorado University for 26 years. He directs Western's MFA in Creative Writing and also teaches undergraduate creative writing. His own works include two collections of poetry (*Wire Song*, 2001; Tamped, *But Loose Enough to Breathe*, 2008) and four novels—three paranormal adventure-comedies co-written with wife Kym O'Connell-Todd (*Little Greed Men*, 2011; *All Plucked Up*, 2012; *The Magicke Outhouse*, 2013) and one science-fiction novel (*Strange Attractors*, 2012). He has two narrative nonfiction books forthcoming in 2015.

Sonya Unrein is the editorial director for Conundrum Press, a literary imprint of Samizdat Publishing Group. She is also a freelance editor, book designer, and publishing consultant for authors and small presses. She has a master's degree from the University of Denver in Digital Media Studies, and lives near Denver with her husband and cat.